It's just fun!
– William Dahlgreen, age 5

After having taught literally hundreds of children to read both as a kindergarten teacher and as a certified reading specialist, I was quite picky in going about how I was going to teach my own children to read. I knew I wanted something phonics-based, open-and-go for me as a parent, and mentally and physically engaging for my young children. I knew I did NOT want a million pieces or parts and books to juggle, and I did not want anything I was going to wind up having to supplement with other pieces, parts, and programs. I found what I really wanted in Logic of English *Foundations*. *Foundations* fully integrates handwriting, phonics, beginning reading, and beginning spelling. There is no need to supplement with other programs. The teacher's manual is well-designed. I didn't need to read through a ton of script to figure out what I was doing that particular day. It has a nice layout. Those parents who really want their hands held in HOW to teach reading will find comfort in this program because everything is there. The activities for the children are fully engaging and can be used as easily with Little Miss Sits Still as well as Mr. Rolls-Around-on-the-Floor. I wish I had Logic of English *Foundations* when I had a classroom of children! But I will settle on using it with my own, knowing that I have seen and tried many programs with many children, and I feel this is absolutely the best program available.

– Lori Archer, M.Ed., Reading Specialist, Homeschool Teacher

The progress in my son's reading and writing abilities in the few months since we began using *Foundations* is truly unbelievable. My son has gone from a very reluctant, struggling reader, to a confident and happy learner. The lessons are well-paced, engaging, and so full of activities and fun that he doesn't notice how much he is learning – but I do.

– Elisa St. Clair, Homeschool Teacher

I have been able to teach my 6th grade dyslexic child, my 4th grade strong reader and my 2nd grade emerging reader all at the same time, and actually enjoy it!

– Kyle Snead Thomas, Homeschool Teacher

Today while playing a reading game my son was giggling and said, "This is awesome!" LOE *Foundations* has made teaching easy and fun. I wish I'd had this program when teaching my other kids!

– Jonie Arends, Homeschool Teacher

This program not only taught my active child to read and write; *Foundations* taught me to work with my active child's natural energy level and interests. Learning together is fun again!

– Heather Aliano, Homeschool Teacher

Today my 5 year old daughter said, "Mom, I love English, you make everything fun!" I cannot put in words how grateful I am for Logic of English. English is not my native tongue and we've struggled with English until we switched to LOE. Now my 5- and 6-year-old daughters plead for LOE. Why not? It is fun (even for me)! Not only is it a program with well laid out instructions for the teacher, it uses all styles of learning so no matter the abilities of the student they will learn.

– Adriana B., Homeschool Mom

I am so thankful to have discovered Logic of English. Teaching my oldest reading was becoming more and more challenging each day. Starting *Foundations* has really changed that for us, and as a bonus my younger daughter was interested, so she has joined in on our teaching time. The program is well laid out and enjoyable to use. Thank you for making me excited to teach English instead of dreading it each day.

– Rachel Walters, Homeschooler

Being new to homeschooling and having struggled with English as a student, I was apprehensive about teaching our children to read. When I came across LOE I knew why I had struggled so much; the phonograms and rules had never been taught to me. As I began to teach my son, not only did he soak up everything, but I found myself learning something new with every lesson. The Logic of English *Foundations* equips parents/teachers with the tools to teach their child how to decode words while making reading fun. Brilliant!

– Erin Stewart, Homeschooling Mom of 3

LOE is a great part of our homeschooling curriculum! It makes learning fun, even for myself as I finally learn why English is the way it is! It should be in every school!

– Trisha Koski

I love learning to write cursive and I love that you get to play games. I love to do school in the morning at our house.

– Bella, age 4

I like the handwriting a lot, because then we can learn cursive. I don't think many 4-year-olds (sister Bella, age 4) and 6-year-olds know cursive. Learning phonograms is fun and you get to do games in it.

– Kaylin, age 6

Foundations

LEVEL B — Teacher's Manual

Denise Eide

LogicofEnglish®

Foundations Level B Teacher's Manual
by Logic of English®

Pedia Learning Inc.
10800 Lyndale Ave S. Suite 181
Minneapolis, MN 55420

Cover Design & Illustration: Ingrid Hess
LOE School Font: David Occhino Design

ISBN 978-1-936706-33-4

First Edition

10 9 8 7 6 5 4 3

www.LogicOfEnglish.com

Lesson	Phonemic Awareness	Phonogram Spelling Rule	Handwriting	Spelling
41	Review short and long vowel sounds.	Learn sh .	Learn uppercase S .	fish, ship, flash, spot, drum
42	Counting syllables.	Learn th .	Learn uppercase T .	this, fit, that, drip, quiz
43	Learn about syllables.	A E O U usually say their long sounds at the end of the syllable.	Learn uppercase F .	he, she, go, so, drop
44	Review syllables.	Sentences begin with an uppercase letter and end with an end mark.	Learn uppercase H .	we, is, thin, had, did
45	Learn about schwa as a lazy vowel sound.		Learn uppercase M .	a, his, the, then, path

Review Lesson A

Lesson	Phonemic Awareness	Phonogram Spelling Rule	Handwriting	Spelling
46	Create new words by changing the first sound.	Learn ck .	Learn uppercase N .	with, duck, quack, math, track
47	Create new words by changing the initial sound.	Two-letter CK is used only after a single, short vowel.	Learn uppercase A .	be, me, shut, rock, shot
48	Practice blending.	Learn igh .	Learn uppercase D .	black, light, night, wish, snack
49	Practice blending.	Learn ch .	Learn uppercase B .	chin, chick, no, bright, bath
50	Review short and long vowel sounds.	Learn ee .	Learn uppercase P .	three, back, see, feel, thick

Review Lesson B

Lesson	Phonemic Awareness	Phonogram Spelling Rule	Handwriting	Spelling
51	Review syllables.	Learn er .	Learn uppercase R .	her, green, sick, feet, check
52	Review syllables. Practice letter names.	Learn wh .	Learn uppercase W .	when, which, get, stand, queen
53	To make a word plural, just add -S.	English words do not end in I, U, V, or J. Learn oi oy .	Learn uppercase U .	boy, coin, feed, joy, bunch

Lesson	Phonemic Awareness	Phonogram Spelling Rule	Handwriting	Spelling
54	Review short and long vowels.	English words do not end in I, U, V, or J. Learn ai ay.	Learn uppercase I .	play, tail, day, sleep, cheer
55	Compare the sounds /f/ and /v/.		Learn uppercase J .	of, as, has, free, click

Review Lesson C

Lesson	Phonemic Awareness	Phonogram Spelling Rule	Handwriting	Spelling
56	Review long and short vowel sounds.	The vowel says its long sound because of the E.		made, name, stop, time, may
57	Review long and short vowel sounds.	Review: the vowel says its long sound because of the E.	Learn uppercase K .	bike, nine, street, grape, high
58	Learn that U has two long vowel sounds.	Review reading questions.	Learn uppercase V .	fire, cute, pick, flute, sheep
59	Review the ways to make a vowel say its long sound.	Silent final E words.	Learn uppercase Y .	like, ride, keep, pink, quick
60	Change the initial sound to form new words.	Learn ng .	Learn uppercase C .	thing, sing, clock, snake, note

Review Lesson D

Lesson	Phonemic Awareness	Phonogram Spelling Rule	Handwriting	Spelling
61	Listen for silent final E's.	English words do not end in V.	Learn uppercase E .	have, give, smile, ask, thank
62	Review the long sounds of U.	English words do not end in U.	Learn uppercase O .	blue, true, must, save, game
63	Review how to spell silent final E words.		Learn uppercase Q .	take, wave, song, drive, glue
64	Learn to rhyme words.	Learn ar .	Learn uppercase G .	car, far, same, jar, ring
65	Practice rhyming words.	Learn or .		or, for, much, gave, sight

Review Lesson E

Lesson	Phonemic Awareness	Phonogram Spelling Rule	Handwriting	Spelling
66	Learn about broad vowel sounds.		Learn uppercase L .	want, wash, to, snail, cave,
67	Explore the broad /ü/ sound.	We often double ff.	Learn uppercase X .	put, off, stuff, star, chair

Lesson	Phonemic Awareness	Phonogram Spelling Rule	Handwriting	Spelling
68	Practice short, long, and broad vowels.	We often double ll.	Learn uppercase Z.	ball, tall, do, tray, trail
69	Practice short, long, and broad vowels.	We often double ss.		class, mess, short, pull, shall
70	Practice rhyming words.	We occasionally double other letters.		egg, buzz, bring, cake, way

Review Lesson F

Lesson	Phonemic Awareness	Phonogram Spelling Rule	Handwriting	Spelling
71	Test multi-letter vowels and consonants.	Learn tch. Three letter /ch/ is used only after a single vowel which says its short or broad sound.		catch, watch, hill, glass, rope
72	Learn strategies for reading phonograms with multiple sounds.	Learn ow.		cow, snow, tell, corn, hatch
73	Learn strategies for reading phonograms with multiple sounds.	Learn ou.		out, round, what, less, sting
74	Learn strategies for reading phonograms with multiple sounds.	Learn ough.		was, thought, that, wall, king
75	Review syllables and plurals.			I, you, your, flour, dough

Review Lesson G

Lesson	Phonemic Awareness	Phonogram Spelling Rule	Handwriting	Spelling
76	Practice rhyming words.			pay, paid, say, said, white
77	Read say, says, and said.			says, down, right, deer, make
78	English words do not end in I, U, V, or J.	Y says long I at the end of a one syllable word.		by, show, fly, pass, ate
79	Learn strategies for reading phonograms with multiple sounds.	Learn ea.		great, my, team, cry, grass
80	Change the initial sound to form new words.	Learn oa.		read, won, boat, coat, head

Review Lesson H

Foundations

Supplies Needed

The materials needed for each activity are listed in a box near the page margin, with optional items in italics. A list is also included at the beginning of each lesson. Teachers should look through each lesson in advance in order to gather the necessary materials. Many lessons include items commonly found in a classroom or home such as crayons, glue, scissors, blocks, a mirror, toy cars, and chalk. In addition to these items, the teacher will need the following:

Foundations B Teacher's Manual
Foundations B Student Workbook - one per student, in either manuscript or cursive
Foundations B Readers
Basic Phonogram Flash Cards
Rhythm of Handwriting Tactile Cards - in either manuscript or cursive
Rhythm of Handwriting Quick Reference - in either manuscript or cursive
Phonogram & Spelling Rule Quick Reference
Spelling Analysis Card
Phonogram Game Cards - two contrasting sets per student or group of four students
Phonogram Game Tiles
LOE Student Whiteboard - one per student, plus whiteboard markers and eraser

Optional:
Rhythm of Handwriting Desk Strip - one per student, in either manuscript or cursive
Phonics with Phonograms App by Logic of English - available at iTunes
Bob Books Set 1 and Set 2, by Bobby Lynn Maslen, Scholastic Inc. 2006. Additional book suggestions for Foundations lessons are available at www.LogicOfEnglish.com/Foundations.

Cursive or Manuscript Handwriting?

Foundations includes instructions for both cursive and manuscript. Before beginning, the teacher should decide which style is best for the student. We suggest all teachers read the article "Why Teach Cursive First" on the Logic of English Blog and consider these questions:

Does the student struggle with fine motor activities? If the student has weak fine motor skills, begin with cursive. Cursive requires significantly less fine motor movement than manuscript. Also, all cursive lowercase letters begin at the same place, on the baseline.

Does the child show signs of reversing letters while reading and/or writing? If the student has demonstrated confusion about the direction of b's and d's or p's and q's, cursive can be very helpful in minimizing the issue. Cursive handwriting naturally emphasizes the direction of reading and writing, and it is difficult to reverse cursive letters.

Does the child attend school where manuscript handwriting is taught? If a parent or tutor is using Foundations to supplement a reading program at school, we suggest matching the handwriting style to that of the school to minimize confusion.

Review Lessons

Every fifth lesson in Foundations is followed by a review and assessment lesson. These lessons provide opportunities to assess the progress of each student and select custom practice activities. At this stage, all students should be taught to the point of mastery. Assessments should not be used to grade students, but rather to determine which skills need further practice.

Each review lesson includes a chart with the skills which have been taught in the previous ten lessons. Skills marked with a 1 should be mastered before the student progresses to the next lesson. Skills marked with a 2 should be familiar to the child, but the child can still be working towards mastery. Level 2 skills will be practiced extensively in the upcoming lessons. Skills with a 3 do not need to be mastered in order for students to progress. Some activities labeled with a 3 are beneficial to some students, but not necessary for all. Other Level 3 skills will be covered extensively in later lessons. Level 3 skills are not included in the assessment activities.

Speech Tips

Some lessons include speech tips for helping students to clearly articulate a phonogram's sound(s). For further ideas we recommend the resource *Eliciting Sounds: Techniques and Strategies for Clinicians 2nd Edition*, by Wayne A. Secord, Cengage Learning 2007.

Spelling Analysis

The process of spelling analysis teaches students to think critically about words rather than memorizing spelling words by rote. With support and guidance from the teacher, students apply the phonograms and rules in new words and analyze why they are spelled the way they are, strengthening both reading and spelling skills.

The steps for spelling analysis are printed on the Spelling Analysis Card and modeled in the first few lessons. Spelling hints and markings for analyzing the words are provided in each spelling list. To learn more, see the free video tutorial "Spelling Dictation: A Multi-Sensory Approach to Reading and Spelling" at www.LogicOfEnglish.com/Video.

Terms

Phonogram – A visual representation of a sound. A phonogram may have one, two, three, or four letters (**p**en, **rai**n, n**igh**t, d**augh**ter). Foundations B teaches students 21 multi-letter phonograms and their sounds. The twenty-six single-letter phonograms are taught in Level A.

CVC Word – A word that follows this pattern: consonant-vowel-consonant.

Pronunciation – Letters that are between two slashes should be referred to by the sound(s). For example, /k/ indicates that you should say the sound /k/, not the letter name "kay."

High Frequency Words – The 300 most frequently used words make up 65% of all that we read and write. Foundations teaches students how to sound out high frequency words and analyze the spelling, rather than memorizing words by rote. A chart of the high frequency words that are explicitly taught in Foundations B can be found on page VI.

HIGH FREQUENCY WORDS

fish	clock	toy	high	rule	to	pink	slow	laid
ship	rock	boy	wheel	base	car	quit	loud	says
spot	truck	feed	club	drove	corn	pass	four	found
swim	shut	joy	fire	way	farm	add	you	by
this	shot	street	white	bone	pull	those	pound	sky
fit	lost	play	lake	came	put	use	count	try
that	light	tail	store	wife	push	small	young	fly
help	night	day	wave	home	full	start	shout	my
them	stick	mail	while	line	off	ate	cloud	dry
think	right	bank	like	blue	here	match	your	why
wish	chick	of	deep	save	fall	catch	out	rich
with	bright	as	hole	broke	ball	watch	round	pitch
we	three	free	sing	solve	tall	water	what	court
me	see	wait	king	take	wall	cow	branch	seat
go	feel	lay	ring	drive	call	how	I	head
no	thick	train	being	cake	bell	now	was	great
he	need	join	bring	main	sell	brown	thought	clean
she	green	paint	thing	pig	well	snow	bought	eat
so	might	chair	song	rain	tell	grow	about	team
then	sheep	note	long	make	do	low	though	coat
is	sleep	rate	string	date	will	town	late	coast
thin	seed	ride	strong	far	its	blow	through	soap
a	her	made	game	star	week	row	left	read
his	feet	name	five	tire	less	show	mix	won
the	check	time	sail	or	miss	crowd	more	boat
path	keep	may	have	for	glass	shine	roll	warm
be	much	hope	give	gave	grass	life	dress	own
sick	pick	tube	thank	sight	class	throw	pay	our
back	nest	rode	live	quite	short	shop	paid	bread
black	tree	past	say	these	shall	down	said	forth
track	when	slide	plain	egg	all	nose	next	close
duck	which	plane	same	want	doll	dark	clerk	air
has	hers	nine	stone	wash	hill			

VI

PHONOGRAMS

a	/ă-ā-ä/	m**a**t	t**a**ble	f**a**ther	
ai	/ā/	l**ai**d			
ar	/är/	c**ar**			
ay	/ā/	pl**ay**			
b	/b/	**b**at			
c	/k-s/	**c**at	**c**ent		
ch	/ch-k-sh/	**ch**ild	s**ch**ool	**ch**ef	
ck	/k/	ba**ck**			
d	/d/	**d**ad			
e	/ĕ-ē/	t**e**nt	b**e**		
ea	/ē-ĕ-ā/	**ea**t	br**ea**d	st**ea**k	
ee	/ē/	tr**ee**			
er	/er/	h**er**			
f	/f/	**f**oot			
g	/g-j/	bi**g**	**g**ym		
h	/h/	**h**at			
i	/ĭ-ī-ē-y/	**i**t	**i**vy	stad**i**um	on**i**on
igh	/ī/	n**igh**t			
j	/j/	**j**ob			
k	/k/	**k**it			
l	/l/	**l**ap			
m	/m/	**m**e			
n	/n/	**n**ut			
ng	/ng/	si**ng**			
o	/ŏ-ō-ö/	**o**n	g**o**	d**o**	
oa	/ō/	c**oa**t			

VII

oi	/oi/	b**oi**l			
or	/or/	l**or**d			
ou	/ow-ō-ö-ŭ/	h**ou**se	s**ou**l	gr**ou**p	c**ou**ntry
ough	/ŏ-ō-ö-ow-ŭf-ŏf/	th**ough**t	th**ough**	thr**ough**	
		b**ough**	r**ough**	tr**ough**	
ow	/ow-ō/	pl**ow**	sn**ow**		
oy	/oi/	b**oy**			
p	/p/	**p**an			
qu	/kw/	**qu**een			
r	/r/	**r**an			
s	/s-z/	**s**ent	a**s**		
sh	/sh/	**sh**e			
t	/t/	**t**ip			
tch	/ch/	bu**tch**er			
th	/th-TH/	**th**in	**th**is		
u	/ŭ-ū-ö-ü/	**u**p	p**u**pil	fl**u**te	p**u**t
v	/v/	**v**an			
w	/w/	**w**all			
wh	/wh/	**wh**isper			
x	/ks-z/	fo**x**	**x**ylophone		
y	/y-ĭ-ī-ē/	**y**ard	g**y**m	b**y**	bab**y**
z	/z/	**z**ip			

Lesson	Needed	Optional
41	LOE whiteboard, Basic Phonogram Flash Card sh , Tactile Card 𝒮 or 𝒮	Rhythm of Handwriting Wall Chart or Classroom Wall Cards or Desk Strip, ABC Song recording, foods, books and activities for "sh" Day, stamp and ink, Phonogram Game Tiles
42	LOE whiteboard, Basic Phonogram Flash Cards A-Z, th , sh , Tactile Card 𝒯 or 𝒯, Phonogram Chart, buzzer, blocks, timer, scissors	Items for "th" Day, music, drum, mirror, Phonogram Game Tiles
43	LOE whiteboard, Tactile Card 𝒯 and 𝒯 or 𝐸, Phonogram Chart, bowl, pennies, Phonogram Cards, red and black dry-erase markers, Phonogram Game Tiles, pennies or tokens for Bingo, space for running	Sensory tray with shaving cream
44	LOE whiteboard, Basic Phonogram Flash Cards, Tactile Card 𝐻 or 𝐻, Phonogram Chart, a children's book, crayons or markers	Phonogram Game Tiles, drum, tape or balance beam, paper for poster, scissors
45	LOE whiteboard, Tactile Card 𝑚 or 𝑀, Phonogram Chart, paper or poster board for a Lazy Vowel Chart, chocolate chips or tokens for Bingo, Reader 1	Phonogram Game Tiles, books from book list
A Review	Basic Phonogram Flash Cards v , x , y , z , sh , th , highlighter, LEGO®'s or blocks	Whiteboard or sensory box
46	LOE whiteboard, Basic Phonogram Flash Card ck , Tactile Card 𝑛 or 𝑁, scissors, Phonogram Game Tiles, Phonogram Chart	
47	LOE whiteboard, Basic Phonogram Flash Cards ck and phonograms learned so far, stop watch, Tactile Card 𝑎 or 𝐴 Phonogram Chart	Phonogram Game Tiles, scissors
48	LOE whiteboard, Phonogram Card igh , Tactile Card 𝒟 or 𝒟, large whiteboard, NERF® gun or small soft ball, small crackers or treats, Phonogram Chart, scissors	Sensory box, Phonogram Game Tiles, books from book list
49	LOE whiteboard, Phonogram Chart, Basic Phonogram Flash Cards learned so far and ch , Tactile Card 𝐵 or 𝐵, three bases and a home plate, scissors, markers or crayons	Highlighter, Phonogram Game Tiles
50	LOE whiteboard, Basic Phonogram Flash Cards learned so far and ee , Phonogram Chart, Tactile Card 𝒫 or 𝒫, Reader 2	Phonogram Game Tiles

Lesson	Needed	Optional
B Review	Basic Phonogram Flash Cards sh, th, ck, igh, ch, ee, highlighter	Whiteboard or sensory box, slips of paper, basket
51	LOE whiteboard, Basic Phonogram Flash Cards er and r, Tactile Card ℛ or R, two decks of Phonogram Game Cards, scissors, a box or basket, bag	Phonogram Game Tiles
52	LOE whiteboard, all the Basic Phonogram Flash Cards learned so far and wh, Tactile Card 𝒲 or W, timer, magnetic upper- and lowercase letters for A, B, D, F, H, M, N, P, R, S, T, cloth bag	Phonogram Game Tiles
53	LOE whiteboard, Phonogram Cards previously learned and oi and oy, Tactile Card 𝒰 or U, timer, blocks	Phonogram Game Tiles, playdough, popsicle stick, objects in the room that represent words
54	LOE whiteboard, Basic Phonogram Flash Cards ay and ai, Tactile Card 𝓘 or I, two sets of Phonogram Game Cards	Sensory box with sand, rice, or cornmeal, Phonogram Game Tiles, highlighter, a book from the book list
55	LOE whiteboard, Tactile Card 𝓙 or J, two sets of Phonogram Game Cards, game board pieces, a red and a green die, Phonogram Chart, Basic Phonogram Flash Cards f and v, Lazy Vowel Chart, Reader 3	Sidewalk chalk, Phonogram Game Tiles, a book from the book list
C Review	Basic Phonogram Flash Cards ck, igh, ch, ee, er, wh, oi, oy, ai, ay, highlighter	Whiteboard or sensory box, index cards, matchbox car, High Frequency Word Cards, Game board 55.3, game pieces, die
56	LOE whiteboard, two sets of Phonogram Game Cards, game board from worksheet 55.3, game pieces, a red and a green die, Phonogram Cards a, e, i, o, u, Phonogram Game Tiles, table, blankets, bag	
57	LOE whiteboard, Tactile Card 𝒦 or K, Bingo game pieces, crayons or markers	Sidewalk chalk, Phonogram Game Tiles
58	LOE whiteboard, Basic Phonogram Flash Card u, Tactile Card 𝒱 or V, Phonogram Game Cards, stop watch, game pieces, scissors	Paper and pencil, Phonogram Game Tiles
59	LOE whiteboard, Tactile Card 𝒴 or Y, two sets of Phonogram Game Cards, game board and words from worksheet 58.3, game pieces, scissors	Phonogram Game Tiles
60	LOE whiteboard, Tactile Card 𝒞 or C, Basic Phonogram Flash Card ng, Phonogram Game Tiles, Bingo game pieces, Reader 4	Crayons or markers, paper
D Review	Basic Phonogram Flash Cards u, er, wh, oi, oy, ai, ay, ng, highlighter	Whiteboard or sensory box

Lesson	Needed	Optional
61	LOE whiteboard, Tactile Card $\mathcal{E}$ or E, two sets of Phonogram Game Cards, Basic Phonogram Flash Card v, scissors, glue, prizes for store	Phonogram Game Tiles, window paint
62	LOE whiteboard, Tactile Card $\mathcal{O}$ or O, Basic Phonogram Flash Card u, two sets of Phonogram Game Cards	Phonogram Game Tiles, scissors
63	LOE whiteboard, Tactile Card $\mathcal{Q}$ or Q, sidewalk chalk or paper plates and markers, Basic Phonogram Flash Cards, beanbag or stone, scissors, Lazy Vowel Chart	Phonogram Game Tiles
64	LOE whiteboard, Basic Phonogram Flash Card ar, two sets of Phonogram Game Cards, timer, cloth bag, Tactile Card $\mathcal{G}$ or G, scissors	Phonogram Game Tiles
65	LOE whiteboard, Basic Phonogram Flash Card or, Bingo tokens such as raisins or pennies, Reader 5	Phonogram Game Tiles, toy cars
E Review	Basic Phonogram Flash Cards ng, ar, or, highlighter	Whiteboard or sensory box
66	LOE whiteboard, Tactile Card $\mathcal{L}$ or L, sensory box filled with sand, Basic Phonogram Flash Cards a, e, o, u, High Frequency Word Cards from lessons 42, 48, 51, 63, scissors, empty ice cream bucket	Phonogram Game Tiles, tray with shaving cream or whipped cream, construction paper and stickers, a book from the book list
67	LOE whiteboard, Phonogram Game Cards, Basic Phonogram Flash Card u, matchbox cars, Tactile Card $\mathcal{X}$ or X, scissors, word bucket, High Frequency Word cards from Lessons 42, 48, 51, 63, 66	Phonogram Game Tiles, window paint, index cards, a book from the book list
68	LOE whiteboard, Tactile Card $\mathcal{Z}$ or Z, 15-20 Basic Phonogram Flash Cards, raisins or tokens for Bingo, timer, scissors, word bucket, Fox cards and Number cards from previous lessons	Phonogram Game Tiles, balance beam or masking tape
69	LOE whiteboard, markers or crayons, finger paint and paper, highlighter, scissors, word bucket, Fox, Number, and Trap cards from previous lessons, timer	Phonogram Game Tiles
70	LOE whiteboard, scissors, two sets of Phonogram Game Cards, word bucket, Fox, Number, Trap, and Timer cards from previous lessons, timer, Reader 6	Phonogram Game Tiles
F Review	Basic Phonogram Flash Cards sh, th, ck, igh, ch, ee, er, wh, oi, oy, ai, ay, ng, ar, or, highlighter	Whiteboard or sensory box

Lesson	Needed	Optional
71	LOE whiteboard, Basic Phonogram Flash Cards `tch`, `igh`, `ng`, `ay`, `ai`, `oy`, `oi`, `ee`, `sh`, `th`, bell, hat, chair, ball, glass of water, toy dog, rug, toy car, shorts, watch, fork	Phonogram Game Tiles, timer, scissors, bucket
72	LOE whiteboard, Basic Phonogram Flash Card `ow`, Phonogram Game Cards, scissors, timer	Phonogram Game Tiles
73	LOE whiteboard, Basic Phonogram Flash Cards `ou` and `ow`, timer, 15 Basic Phonogram Flash Cards to practice, pennies or tokens for Bingo, Lazy Vowel Chart	Phonogram Game Tiles, scissors, a book from the book list
74	LOE whiteboard, Basic Phonogram Flash Card `ough`, blocks or LEGO®s, Lazy Vowel Chart, playdough, alphabet cookie cutters, stick, scissors	Phonogram Game Tiles, books from book list
75	LOE whiteboard, two sets of Phonogram Game Cards, timer, cloth bag, Reader 7	Phonogram Game Tiles
G **Review**	Basic Phonogram Flash Cards `tch`, `ow`, `ou`, `ough`, highlighter	Index cards
76	LOE whiteboard, Basic Phonogram Flash Cards, red and black dry-erase markers, scissors	Phonogram Game Tiles, large whiteboard, small soft ball, NERF® gun with suction cup darts, index cards
77	LOE whiteboard, scissors, Basic Phonogram Flash Cards, buzzer, word bucket	Phonogram Game Tiles, toy car
78	LOE whiteboard, Basic Phonogram Flash Card `y`, large whiteboard, small soft ball	Phonogram Game Tiles, scissors, NERF® gun with suction cup darts
79	LOE whiteboard, Basic Phonogram Flash Card `ea`, two sets of Phonogram Game Cards, a list of High Frequency Words from Lessons 42, 48, 51, 63, 66-70, 77	Phonogram Game Tiles, scissors
80	LOE whiteboard, Basic Phonogram Flash Cards learned so far and `oa`, Phonogram Game Tiles, 3 bases and a home plate, Lazy Vowel Chart, scissors, Reader 8	
H **Review**	Basic Phonogram Flash Cards `tch`, `ow`, `ou`, `ough`, `ea`, `oa`, highlighter	Whiteboard, small soft ball or NERF® gun with suction cup darts

Common Core Standards

Standard		Foundations A - B Lessons
Kindergarten **Reading Foundational Skills**		
RF.K.1a	Follow words from left to right, top to bottom, and page by page.	21-80
RF.K.1b	Recognize that spoken words are represented in written language by specific sequences of letters.	21-80
RF.K.1c	Understand that words are separated by spaces in print.	27-80
RF.K.1d	Recognize and name all upper- and lowercase letters of the alphabet.	5-68
RF.K.2a	Recognize and produce rhyming words.	64-65, 70, 76, 78-79
RF.K.2b	Count, pronounce, blend, and segment syllables in spoken words.	42-44, 51-52, 75
RF.K.2c	Blend and segment onsets and rimes of single-syllable spoken words.	3-10
RF.K.2d	Isolate and pronounce the initial, medial vowel, and final sounds (phonemes) in three-phoneme (consonant-vowel-consonant, or CVC) words.	7-9, 11-12, 15, 17-29, 31-32
RF.K.2e	Add or substitute individual sounds (phonemes) in simple, one-syllable words to make new words.	33-34, 46-47, 60, 80
RF.K.3a	Demonstrate basic knowledge of one-to-one letter-sound correspondences by producing the primary sound or many of the most frequent sounds for each consonant.	6-40
RF.K.3b	Associate the long and short sounds with the common spellings (graphemes) for the five major vowels.	5-40
RF.K.3c	Read common high frequency words by sight (e.g. the, of, to, you, she, my, is, are, do, does).	42-80
RF.K.3d	Distinguish between similarly spelled words by identifying the sounds of the letters that differ.	77
RF.K.4	Read emergent-reader texts with purpose and understanding.	25, 30, 35, 40, 45, 50, 55, 60, 65, 70, 75, 80
First Grade **Reading Foundational Skills**		
RF.1.1a	Recognize the distinguishing features of a sentence (e.g. first word, capitalization, ending punctuation).	44
RF.1.2a	Distinguish long from short vowel sounds in spoken single-syllable words.	36-39, 41, 50, 54, 56-59, 61-62, 68-69
RF.1.2b	Orally produce single-syllable words by blending sounds (phonemes), including consonant blends.	3-80 (This skill is practiced through spelling dictation.)

Standard		Foundations A - B Lessons
RF.1.2c	Isolate and pronounce initial, medial vowel, and final sounds (phonemes) in spoken single-syllable words.	7-9, 11-12, 15, 17-29, 31-32
RF.1.2d	Segment spoken single-syllable words into their complete sequence of individual sounds (phonemes).	10-80 (This skill is practiced through spelling dictation.)
RF.1.3a	Know the spelling-sound correspondences for common consonant digraphs.	41-80 (Introduced throughout and practiced daily with phonogram games.)
RF.1.3b	Decode regularly spelled one-syllable words.	21-120
RF.1.3c	Know final -e and common vowel team conventions for representing long vowel sounds.	48-80 (Introduced throughout and practiced daily with phonogram games and silent E games.)
RF.1.3d	Use knowledge that every syllable must have a vowel sound to determine the number of syllables in a printed word.	Foundations Level C
RF.1.3e	Decode two-syllable words following basic patterns by breaking the words into syllables.	Foundations Level C
RF.1.3f	Read words with inflectional endings.	Foundations Level C
RF.1.3g	Recognize and read grade-appropriate irregularly spelled words.	45, 55, 66-67, 76
RF.1.4a	Read grade-level text with purpose and understanding.	25, 30, 35, 40, 45, 50, 55, 60, 65, 70, 75, 80
RF.1.4b	Read grade-level text orally with accuracy, appropriate rate, and expression on successive readings.	25, 30, 35, 40, 45, 50, 55, 60, 65, 70, 75, 80
RF.1.4c	Use context to confirm or self-correct word recognition and understanding, rereading as necessary.	80
Kindergarten Language Skills		
L.K.1a	Print many upper- and lowercase letters.	5-68
L.K.1b	Use frequently occurring nouns and verbs.	1-80
L.K.1c	Form regular plural nouns orally by adding /s/ or /es/ (e.g. dog, dogs; wish, wishes).	53, 57, 75
L.K.1d	Understand and use question words (interrogatives) (e.g. who, what, where, when, why, how).	52, 58, 74, 77
L.K.1e	Use the most frequently occurring prepositions (e.g. to, from, in, out, on, off, for, of, by, with).	24, 47, 49, 54, 59, 62, 64, 69, 71, 72, 73, 78
L.K.1f	Produce and expand complete sentences in shared language activities.	1-80
L.K.2a	Capitalize the first word in a sentence and the pronoun I.	44, 75
L.K.2b	Recognize and name end punctuation.	44
L.K.2c	Write a letter or letters for most consonant and short-vowel sounds (phonemes).	5-80
L.K.2d	Spell simple words phonetically, drawing on knowledge of sound-letter relationships.	21-80
L.K.4a	Identify new meanings for familiar words and apply them accurately (e.g. knowing duck is a bird and learning the verb to duck).	1, 23

Standard		Foundations A - B Lessons
L.K.4b	Use the most frequently occurring inflections and affixes (e.g. -ed, -s, re-, un-, pre-, -ful, -less) as a clue to the meaning of an unknown word.	53
L.K.5a	Sort common objects into categories (e.g. shapes, foods) to gain a sense of the concepts the categories represent.	41, 43-45, 47, 53-54, 56, 58-59, 61-67, 70-71, 77
L.K.5b	Demonstrate understanding of frequently occurring verbs and adjectives by relating them to their opposites (antonyms).	50, 52, 55-56, 59, 66, 68, 72
L.K.5c	Identify real-life connections between words and their use (e.g. note places at school that are colorful).	50, 53-54, 56-65, 69-73, 75-77
L.K.5d	Distinguish shades of meaning among verbs describing the same general action (e.g. walk, march, strut, prance) by acting out the meanings.	6, 7, 44, 68
L.K.6	Use words and phrases acquired through conversations, reading and being read to, and responding to texts.	45-46, 50, 55, 60-61, 65, 70-71, 75-76, 78-80
Kindergarten Reading Literature		
RL.K.1	With prompting and support, ask and answer questions about key details in a text.	45, 50, 55, 60, 65, 70, 75, 80
RL.K.2	With prompting and support, retell familiar stories, including key details.	45, 50, 55, 60, 65, 70, 75, 80
RL.K.3	With prompting and support, identify characters, settings, and major events in a story.	45, 50, 55, 60, 65, 70, 75, 80
RL.K.4	Ask and answer questions about unknown words in a text.	45, 50, 55, 60, 65, 70, 75, 80
RI.K.5	Recognize common types of texts (e.g. storybooks, poems).	Foundations Level C or as modeled by the teacher
RL.K.6	With prompting and support, name the author and illustrator of a story and define the role of each in telling the story.	45, 50, 55, 60, 65, 70, 75, 80
RL.K.7	With prompting and support, describe the relationship between illustrations and the story in which they appear (e.g. what moment in a story an illustration depicts).	60, 75
RL.K.9	With prompting and support, compare and contrast the adventures and experiences of characters in familiar stories.	55
RL.K.10	Actively engage in group reading activities with purpose and understanding.	45, 50, 55, 60, 65, 70, 75, 80

Kindergarten Writing skills are not addressed in Foundations Levels A & B.

Kindergarten Reading Informational Texts skills are taught in Foundations Level C, and can be modeled by the teacher with informational read-alouds.

COMMON CORE STANDARDS

Lesson	Standards	Lesson	Standards
41	RF.K.1d, RF.1.3a, RF.K.3b, L.K.5a	61	RF.K.1d, RF.1.3b, RF.1.3c, L.K.5a, L.K.5c, L.K.6
42	RF.K.1d, RF.1.3a, RF.K.2b	62	RF.K.1d, RF.1.3c, RF.2.3a, L.K.5a, L.K.5c
43	RF.K.1d, RF.K.2e, RF.1.2b, RF.K.3c, RF.1.2c, RF.K.3b, L.K.5a	63	RF.K.1d, RF.1.3c, RF.2.3a, L.K.5c
44	RF.K.1a, RF.K.1d, RF.1.1a, RF.K.3c, L.K.5a	64	RF.K.1d, RF.K.2a, RF.2.3b, L.K.5a, L.K.5c
45	RF.K.1d, L.K.5a, L.K.6, RL.K.1, RL.K.3	65	RF.K.2a, RL.K.1, RF.K.3c, L.K.5a, L.K.5c, L.K.6, RL.K.3
46	RF.K.1d, RF.K.2c, RF.K.2e, L.K.6, RF.1.3a	66	RF.K.1d, RF.1.3g, L.K.5a, L.K.5b
47	RF.K.1d, RF.K.2c, RF.K.3b, RF.1.2b, L.K.5a	67	RF.K.1d, RF.K.3c, L.K.5a
48	RF.K.1d, RF.K.2c, RF.K.3b, RF.1.2b, RF.1.3c	68	RF.K.1d, RF.K.3b, RF.1.3g, L.K.5b
49	RF.K.1d, RF.K.2c, RF.K.3b, RF.1.2b, RF.1.3a	69	RF.K.3b, L.K.5c
50	RF.K.1d, RF.K.2c, RF.K.3b, RF.1.2b, RF.1.3c, L.K.5b, L.K.5c, L.K.6, RL.K.1, RL.K.3	70	RL.K.1, RF.K.2a, L.K.5a, L.K.5c, L.K.6, RL.K.3
51	RF.K.1d, RF.K.2c, RF.K.3b, RF.1.2b, RF.2.3b	71	RF.1.3a, RF.1.3c, RF.2.3b, L.K.5a, L.K.5c, L.K.6
52	RF.K.1d, RF.K.3a, RF.K.3b, RF.K.2b, RF.1.3a, L.K.5b	72	RF.1.3, RF.2.3b, L.K.5b, L.K.5c
53	RF.K.1d, L.K.1c, L.K.5a, L.K.5c, RF.2.3b	73	RF.1.3, RF.1.3g, RF.2.3b, RF.2.3e, L.K.2.a-b
54	RF.K.1d, RF.K.3b, RF.1.2b, RF.1.3c, L.K.5a, L.K.5c	74	RF.1.3g, RF.2.3b, RF.2.3e, L.K.2.a-b
55	RF.K.1d, RF.K.2c, RF.1.2b, RF.1.2d, RF.K.2, L.K.5b, L.K.6, RL.K.1, RL.K.3	75	RL.K.1, RF.K.3c, L.K.1c, L.K.5c, L.K.6, RL.K.3
56	RF.K.3b, RF.K.2c, RF.1.2b, RF.1.3c, RF.K.2e, L.K.5a, L.K.5b, L.K.5c	76	RF.K.2a, RF.1.3g, L.K.2, L.K.5c, L.K.6
57	RF.K.1d, RF.K.2c, RF.1.2b, L.K.1c, L.K.5c, RF.1.3c	77	RF.K.3d, L.K.5a
58	RF.K.1d, RF.K.2c, RF.1.2b, RF.K.3b, L.K.1d, L.K.5a, L.K.5c	78	RF.K.2a, RF.1.3b, L.K.6
59	RF.K.1d, RF.K.2c, RF.1.2b, RF.1.3c, L.K.5a, L.K.5b, L.K.5c	79	RF.K.2a, RF.2.3b, L.K.6
60	RF.K.1d, RF.1.3a, RF.K.2c, RF.1.2b, RF.K.2e, L.K.5c, L.K.6, RL.K.1, RL.K.3	80	RF.K.2e, RF.1.3g, RF.2.3b, L.K.6, RL.K.1, RL.K.3

BEFORE YOU BEGIN

Objectives

PHONEMIC AWARENESS: Review the definition of a vowel. Review short and long vowel sounds.

Materials

NEEDED: Basic Phonogram Flash Cards or Phonogram Game Cards a , c , d , e , f , g , i , j , o , p , qu , u

OPTIONAL: Basic Phonogram Flash Cards A-Z, LOE whiteboard

For Students New to Foundations

Vowels: Sounds You Can Sing

Today we will test phonograms and put them into groups called vowels and consonants.

The first type of phonogram is called a vowel. It is a sound you can sing and your mouth is open.

Let's test the phonograms and decide if they are vowels.

Show a .

Can you sing the first sound /ă/? */ăăă/, yes*
Is your mouth open as you say the sound? *yes*
Then it is a vowel.

Can you sing the second sound /ā/? */āāā/, yes*
Is your mouth open as you say the sound? *yes*
Then it is a vowel.

Can you sing the third sound /ä/? */äää/, yes*
Is your mouth open as you say the sound? *yes*
Then it is a vowel.

Basic Phonogram Flash Cards or Phonogram Game Cards a c d e f g j o p qu u

Multi-Sensory Fun

Select these phonograms from the Phonogram Game Cards and hand them to the students. Have them sort the cards into a vowel pile and a consonant pile.

Challenge

Provide students with a stack of all the single-letter Basic Phonogram Cards A-Z. Divide the whiteboard in half. Ask students to read each phonogram, then write vowels on one half of the whiteboard and consonants on the other half.

Show ⬚ d .
  Can you sing /d/? *no*
  What is blocking the sound? *my tongue*
  So can this be a vowel? *no*
  /d/ is a consonant sound.

  A consonant is a sound that is blocked by some part of your mouth, such as your tongue, lips, or teeth. Also you cannot sing a consonant sound.

  Let's test the rest of our sounds and decide if they are consonants or vowels.

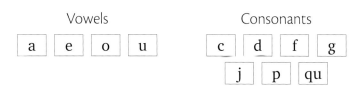

Vowels				Consonants			
a	e	o	u	c	d	f	g
				j	p	qu	

Speech Tip

Some students will mistakenly add the sound /ŭ/ to the /d/ and say /dŭ/ rather than isolating the /d/ sound. In this case they will claim to be able to sing /d/ when in reality they are singing /ŭ/. Help them to hear the difference by singing /ŭ/ then saying /d/ and comparing the two sounds.

Teacher Tip

QU says /kw/. Q always needs a U; U is not a vowel here. It is part of the consonant blend.

Short Vowels

  Have you ever noticed that all the vowels make more than one sound?

  Each of the vowel sounds has a name. The first vowel sound is called the short sound. Let's read the vowels but read only the short sounds.

Show the Phonogram Card a .
  /ă/

Show the Phonogram Card e .
  /ĕ/

Show the Phonogram Card i .
  /ĭ/

Show the Phonogram Card o .
  /ŏ/

Show the Phonogram Card u .
  /ŭ/

  Now I will show you how to mark the short vowel sound. We write a curved line over it. This is called a breve.

Basic Phonogram Flash Cards

a	e	i	o	u

Teacher Tip

Students who are beginning Foundations with Level B will need to become familiar with the difference between long and short vowels. Use this lesson to introduce the concept.

Vocabulary

Breve means short. This root is also found in words such as: abbreviate (to shorten), abbreviation (a shortened form), and brevity (a short time).

Write ă.   Write ĭ.   Write ŭ.
/ă/   /ĭ/   /ŭ/
Write ĕ.   Write ŏ.
/ĕ/   /ŏ/

Let's read the short vowel sounds. While we read them, put your hands over your head in a curved shape like the marking for the short sound.

Point to the short vowels on the board as you read them aloud.

Long Vowels

Which vowel sounds are short? *the first sound of each vowel*
How do we mark them? *put a curved line over them*

The second sound of each vowel is called the long sound. Let's try to read the phonograms, but only say the second sound out loud.

> **Teacher Tip**
>
> U has two long sounds, /ū/ and /ö/. These can be heard by comparing words such as *cute* and *flute*. When we compare the sounds made in these words, we discover that /ū/ and /ö/ are very similar. The only difference is that the initial sound /y/ is dropped for /ö/.

Show the Phonogram Card a .
/ā/

Show the Phonogram Card e .   Show the Phonogram Card o .
/ē/   /ō/

Show the Phonogram Card i .   Show the Phonogram Card u .
/ī/   /ū/

Did you know you just read the names for each of these phonograms? All the single letter phonograms also have a name. For the vowels, the name is the same as the long sound. Now I will show you how to mark the long vowel sound. Write a straight line over it.

I will write the long vowels on the board. Read each sound.

Write ā.   Write ī.   Write ū.
/ā/   /ī/   /ū/
Write ē.   Write ō.
/ē/   /ō/

Let's read the long vowel sounds. While we read them, hold your arms out in a straight line like the marking for the long sound.

Point to the long vowels on the board as you read them aloud.

Objectives

PHONEMIC AWARENESS: Review short and long vowel sounds.

MULTI-LETTER PHONOGRAM: Learn sh .

HANDWRITING: Learn uppercase S .

SPELLING: fish, ship, flash, spot, drum

Materials

NEEDED: LOE whiteboard, Basic Phonogram Flash Card sh , Tactile Card 𝒮 or 𝒮

OPTIONAL: ABC Song recording; Phonogram Wall Chart, Rhythm of Handwriting Desk Strip, or Rhythm of Handwriting Wall Cards; foods, books and activities for "sh" Day; stamp and ink; Phonogram Game Tiles

Phonemic Awareness

Vowels

Write the vowels ā ē ī ō ū ă ĕ ĭ ŏ ŭ on the board in a random order and in a variety of colors.

As I write a vowel sound, read it aloud to me.

Now I will point to a phonogram. Read the sound. As you read it, stretch your arms into a long line if it is the long sound and curve your hands over your head if it is the short sound.

> **Multi-Sensory Fun**
>
> Play "Buzz the Teacher." Tell the student to point to a sound. You should read it. If you are right, the student points to the next sound. If you are wrong, the student should indicate you are wrong by saying "bzzz." Be sure to read a lot of them wrong. Kids love to correct the teacher!

ABC Song

41.1 Phonogram Desk Chart – page 1

Show the students 41.1 Phonogram Desk Chart, or use the Phonogram Wall Chart.

What do you see on the chart? *I see all the phonograms I have learned and some other letters next to them.*

Each of the single-letter phonograms has two ways to write it. The ones we have learned already are called

41.1 Phonogram Desk Chart
ABC Song recording

the lowercase letters. The ones next to them are the uppercase letters, which we sometimes call the capital letters.

Point to a lowercase letter.

Why do you think we call this the lowercase? *It is smaller and sits lower on the lines.*

Point to an uppercase letter.

Why do you think this is called the uppercase? *It is bigger.*

Notice how all the uppercase letters touch the top line. It is as if they live in the upper story.

As I point to each phonogram, let's read the sounds it makes.

Point to Aa.

/ă-ā-ä/

Point to Bb.

/b/...

Each of the single letter phonograms also has a name. We will begin to learn the names by singing the ABC Song. As I sing the ABC Song, I will point to the phonograms. The song is about the phonogram names.

Play a recording of the well-known ABC song, or sing it for the students. Point to each phonogram as you sing its name. Ask the students to sing along if they know the song. Sing the song again.

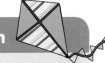

Teacher Tip

Most lessons call for a phonogram chart to practice the alphabet. You may wish to laminate the Phonogram Desk Chart page from the student workbook to use it throughout Foundations B. Other handwriting charts are available at the Logic of English store.

Multi-Sensory Fun

Point to a phonogram. Ask the student to crouch down low if it is lowercase, and stretch up high if it is uppercase.

Handwriting

Teacher Tip

Some teachers may choose to teach the manuscript uppercase letters rather than the cursive to emerging writers. The cursive uppercase letters have more variation in shape, and sometimes are more complex to write.

The goal of teaching the uppercase letters is familiarity. We want students to master writing the lowercase letters and master how to read the uppercase letters. However, they do not need to master how to write the uppercase letters at this level. It is helpful to have a handwriting chart on the wall for reference when students are writing.

Writing Uppercase $\boxed{S}$

41.2 Uppercase S – page 2

Look at the blue and green letters in your workbook. The first two show how upper- and lowercase /s-z/ will appear in

Whiteboard

Tactile Card or $\boxed{S}$

books. What do you notice? *The uppercase and lowercase /s-z/ look the same, but the uppercase is bigger.*

The next two are how we write /s-z/. What do you notice? *Cursive – The uppercase /s-z/ is bigger, and it has a loop on the top. It still has a scoop. The uppercase /s-z/ looks more like the cursive lowercase /s-z/ than like the one we see in books. Manuscript – The manuscript /s-z/ looks like the bookface version.*

Let's learn how to write the uppercase /s-z/.

Demonstrate how to write /s-z/ using the Tactile Card or S .

Start at the baseline. ①**Loop** up to the top line, ②**down** to the midline, ③**scoop** around past the baseline, ④**glide** across.

Start just below the top line. ①**Roll** around to the midline, ②**curve** back past the baseline.

Practice writing the uppercase /s-z/ three times on the Tactile Card or in the air, using your pointer finger.

Shout the directions as you write it on your whiteboard.
Whisper the directions as you write it on your whiteboard.
Sing the directions as you write it on your whiteboard.

Which one sits on the baseline the best?
Which one goes up and touches the top line the best?
Which one looks most like the Tactile Card?
Put a smiley face next to the best /s-z/.

Teacher Tip

Classroom teachers might not have a copy of the Tactile Cards for each student. In this case, demonstrate how to write the letter using the Tactile Card. Ask the students to repeat the steps on their whiteboards using the side with large lines and their pointer finger.

Writing on Paper

41.2 Uppercase S – page 2

Write uppercase /s-z/ three times on your favorite line size.
Circle your favorite uppercase /s-z/.

The Phonogram sh

The Phonogram sh

Show the Phonogram Card sh .
This says /sh/. What does it say? */sh/*

Basic Phonogram Flash Card sh
Whiteboard

How many letters are used to write /sh/? *two*

Write /sh/ three times on your whiteboard.

sh Day

Look at shells. Sail ships. Make shakes. Eat shortcake, shortbread, shish kabobs, and shredded cheese. Learn about shamrocks, shooting stars, sharks, sheep, shrews, shrimp, and sheepdogs. Shampoo doll's hair. Learn the names of shapes. Wear shirts, shorts, and shoes.

Phonogram Practice

Phonogram Tic-Tac-Toe

41.3 Tic-Tac-Toe – pages 3-4

Decide who will play X's and who will play O's. One person chooses a phonogram and reads the sound(s) aloud. If he reads it correctly, he may place an X or an O on the square. Proceed as if playing Tic-Tac-Toe until someone places three in a row or a tie is declared.

Multi-Sensory Fun

Provide each player with a stamp and ink to use on the Tic-Tac-Toe boards instead of writing X's and O's.

Spelling

Spelling List

Teach the words in the list on the next page, using the steps for Spelling Analysis. Direct students to write the words on their whiteboards or with Phonogram Game Tiles.

Spelling Analysis involves teaching the spelling of a word by guiding students in hearing and segmenting its sounds, supporting them with any needed clarification as they use their knowledge of the phonograms to write it, and finally analyzing the spelling together.

The steps are modeled for you with the word *fish*, below. They are also listed for teacher reference on the Spelling Analysis Card (skip steps 3-4 until syllables are introduced in lesson 42). In the rest of the lessons, sample scripting is provided as a resource for difficult words.

Whiteboard
or Phonogram Game Tiles

Teacher Tip

Use finger spelling to cue when to use a multi-letter phonogram. For example, hold up one finger for F, one finger for I, and two fingers for SH.

Word	Sentence	Say to Spell	Markings	Spelling Hints
1. fish	*We caught two fish.*	fĭsh	fi<u>sh</u>	Underline /sh/.
2. ship	*The ship sailed across the ocean.*	shĭp	<u>sh</u>ip	Underline /sh/.
3. flash	*I saw a bright flash.*	flăsh	fla<u>sh</u>	Underline /sh/.
4. spot	*This shirt has a spot on it.*	spŏt	spot	All first sounds.
5. drum	*The drum is very loud.*	drŭm	drum	All first sounds.

fish

The first word is *fish*. We caught two fish. *fish*
Now it is your turn to say "fish," then sound it out.
fish /f-ĭ-sh/

Write *fish* on your whiteboard. As you write it, say each of the sounds aloud. */f-ĭ-sh/*
The student writes *fish* on his whiteboard, saying */f-ĭ-sh/*.

It is now my turn to write *fish*. Drive my marker by sounding it out. */f-ĭ-sh/*
The student sounds out */f-ĭ-sh/* while the teacher writes the word on the board.

When we have two letters working together to say one sound, we will underline the phonogram. Let's underline /sh/.

$$\underline{f\,i\underline{sh}}$$

Let's read it together. Point to each phonogram as you read it. Then blend the word together.
/f-ĭ-sh/ fish

Reading Practice

41.4 Matching – pages 5-6

Match the words to the pictures.

Objectives

PHONEMIC AWARENESS: Counting syllables.

PHONOGRAM: Learn th .

HANDWRITING: Learn uppercase T .

SPELLING: this, fit, that, drip, quiz

Materials

NEEDED: LOE whiteboard, Basic Phonogram Flash Cards A-Z, th , sh , Tactile Card 𝒯 or 𝐸 , Phonogram Chart, buzzer, blocks, timer, scissors

OPTIONAL: Items for "th" Day, music, drum, mirror, Phonogram Game Tiles

The Phonogram th

The Phonogram th

Show the Phonogram Card th .

This says /th-ŀH/. What does it say? */th-TH/*
How many letters are used to write /th-TH/? *two*

Say /th/ and /TH/. What is the same about how you say these sounds? *My mouth is in the same position. I put my tongue under my teeth and blow.*
Why do they sound different? *My voice box is on for /TH/ and off for /th/.*

Write /th-TH/ three times on your whiteboard.
Which one is the neatest? Put a smiley face by it.

Basic Phonogram Flash Card th
Whiteboard

Teacher Tip

/th/ represents the unvoiced sound found in *thin, think,* and *thought*.
/TH/ represents the voiced sound found in *this, these,* and *that*.

Speech Tip

If a student is struggling to say the sound /th/, tell the student to begin by saying /s/. While saying /s/, slowly move the tongue forward until it is touching the bottom of the top teeth. To aid the student in saying /TH/, begin with /z/.

Learn to read a thermometer. Measure the thickness of various books. Count to thirteen and thirty. Learn about thunderstorms. Have a thumb war. Read about the first Thanksgiving. Give thanks!

Phonogram Practice

Teacher Trouble

Have the student quiz the teacher on reading the phonograms. The teacher should make several "mistakes." When the teacher makes a mistake, the student can ring a buzzer.

Basic Phonogram Flash Cards A-Z, | sh |
and | th |
Whiteboard
Buzzer

Handwriting

Writing Uppercase | T |

Whiteboard
Tactile Card ꟼ or Ŧ

42.1 Uppercase T – page 7

In your workbook you will see an uppercase and lowercase /t/ as it is printed in books, and a handwritten uppercase and lowercase /t/. What do you notice about the first two? *The uppercase /t/ is taller and the top sides bend down. The uppercase /t/ has a base that it is standing on. The uppercase /t/ is crossed at the top. The lowercase /l/ has a curve on the bottom and the cross is not at the top.*

The last two are how we write /t/. What do you notice? *Cursive – The uppercase /t/ is taller. It has a scoop at the bottom. The top line has a swerve. Manuscript – The uppercase /t/ is taller. The line is across the top. The lowercase /t/ has the line across the middle.*

Let's learn how to write the uppercase /t/.

Demonstrate how to write /t/ using ꟼ or Ŧ .

 *Start just below the top line.*
①**Slash** down to the baseline,
②**scoop** up to halfway between
the baseline and the midline,
③**glide** across, ④pick up the
pencil, ⑤**swerve** at the top.

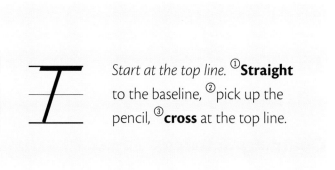 *Start at the top line.* ①**Straight**
to the baseline, ②pick up the
pencil, ③**cross** at the top line.

Write uppercase /t/ three times on the Tactile Card or in the air, using your pointer finger.

Write uppercase /t/ three times on the whiteboard.
Which one looks most like the Tactile Card?
Put a smiley face next to the best /t/.

Writing on Paper

42.1 Uppercase T – page 7

Write uppercase /t/ three times on your favorite line size.
Circle your favorite uppercase /t/.

42.2 Matching Phonograms – page 8

Match the handwritten and bookface letters.

Phonemic Awareness

ABC Song

Sing the ABC song as we point to each of the phonograms.

Phonogram Chart

Music

Drum

Mirror

Counting Syllables

What is a vowel? *A vowel can be sung while the mouth is open.*

What kind of sound is blocked? *consonant*

When you open your mouth to say a vowel and then close it in some way to say a consonant, it makes a beat.

Show your hands opening and then coming together and clapping.

Words have beats. The beats in words are called syllables. We can count the syllables in words by feeling how many times our mouths open to say the vowel sound.

Place your hand under you chin. I will say a word, and you say it back. Feel how many times your mouth opens when you say the word.

bookshelf   *bookshelf two syllables*
baby   *baby two syllables*
man   *man one syllable*
pinecone   *pinecone two syllables*
slide   *slide one syllable*
pen   *pen one syllable*

Multi-Sensory Fun

Before teaching syllables, play music with a strong beat. March, clap, dance, and pound on drums. Feel the beat.

Have students look in a mirror while saying the words. Ask them to count the number of times their mouth opens and closes.

Spelling

Spelling List

Teach the words using the steps for Spelling Analysis. Direct students to write the words on their whiteboards or with Phonogram Game Tiles.

Word	Sentence	Say to Spell	Markings	Spelling Hints
1. this	*This is my new sweater.*	THĭs	²<u>th</u>is	Underline /TH/. Put a 2 over it. /th-TH/ said its second sound.
2. fit	*Do those pants fit?*	fĭt	fit	All first sounds.
3. that	*That pan is hot.*	THăt	²<u>th</u>at	Underline /TH/. Put a 2 over it. /th-TH/ said its second sound.
4. drip	*Wipe up the drip of water.*	drĭp	drip	All first sounds.
5. quiz	*We will have a math quiz tomorrow.*	kwĭz	<u>qu</u>iz	Underline the /kw/.

this

The first word is *this*. This is my new sweater. *this*
Place your hand under your chin and say, "this." How many syllables are in *this*? ***this, one***
Let's sound out *this*   */TH-ĭ-s/*
Now write *this*.
The student writes *this* on her whiteboard.

It is now my turn to write *this*. Sound it out as I write it. */TH-ĭ-s/*
Do you see two letters working together to say one sound? */TH/*
Underline /TH/. Which sound of /th-TH/ is it? ***second***
To remind us /th-TH/ is saying its second sound, we will write a 2 over it.
Let's sound it out together */TH-ĭ-s/* ***this***

that

The next word is *that*. That pan is hot. *that*
Place your hand under your chin and say, "that." How many syllables are in *that*? ***that, one***
Let's sound out *that*. */TH-ă-t/*
Now write *that*.
The student writes *that* on her whiteboard.

It is now my turn to write *that*. Sound it out as I write it. */TH-ă-t/*
Do you see two letters working together to say one sound? */TH/*
Underline /TH/. Which sound of /th-TH/ is it? *second*
To remind us /th-TH/ is saying its second sound, we will write a 2 over it.
Let's sound it out together. */TH-ă-t/ that*

Reading

High Frequency Word Race

42.3 Fluency Practice – pages 9-10

Cut out the words. Put them in a pile face down. Set a timer for two minutes.

Draw a word. Read it aloud. For each word you read correctly place a block on the tower.

Repeat.

Challenge the student to try again and see if he can read more words in two minutes this time.

Scissors
Timer
Blocks

Teacher Tip

Save the high frequency word cards for use in later lessons. We suggest laminating only the high frequency word cards for repeated use.

Classroom High Frequency Word Race

42.3 Fluency Practice – pages 9-10

Cut out the words. Put them in a pile face down. Ask the students to form a line. Assign one student to put the blocks on the tower. Set a timer for two minutes.

Ask the first student to draw a word, then read it aloud. When he reads it correctly have the student add a block to the tower. The next student reads the next word… How many words can the class read in two minutes?
Repeat.

Scissors
Timer
Blocks

Teacher Tip

High frequency words are listed in a chart in the introduction to this book. By reading the first column from top to bottom, then the second column, etc., you will see the order these words are introduced in the lessons. Students have already encountered seven high frequency words before playing this game.

Teacher Tip

This activity also teaches graphing.

Objectives

PHONEMIC AWARENESS: Learn about syllables.

SPELLING RULE: A E O U usually say their long sounds at the end of the syllable.

HANDWRITING: Learn uppercase ⬚F⬚ .

SPELLING: he, she, go, so, drop

Materials

NEEDED: LOE whiteboard, Tactile Card ⬚𝓕⬚ and ⬚𝓕⬚ or ⬚E⬚ , Phonogram Chart, bowl, pennies, Basic Phonogram Flash Cards, red and black dry-erase markers, Phonogram Game Tiles, pennies or tokens for Bingo, space for running

OPTIONAL: Sensory tray with shaving cream

Phonemic Awareness

Syllables

43.1 Syllables and Pictures – page 11

In the last lesson we learned about syllables. How do we count how many syllables are in a word? *Feel how many times our mouth opens to say a vowel.*

Today you have a set of pictures. Circle the pictures that have two syllables. Put an X on the pictures that have one syllable.

baby	pencil
basket	sun
book	flag
cow	flower

Teacher Tip

Syllables are a difficult concept for some students. If the child is struggling with it, do not be concerned. There will be a lot of practice in future lessons.

Multi-Sensory Fun

If the student struggles to hear and feel the syllables, say each of these words by saying the first syllable loudly and the second syllable softly.

ABC Song

Sing the ABC song as we point to each of the phonograms.

Phonogram Chart

Phonogram Practice

Phonogram Arcade Race

Designate a "track." Drop 2-5 pennies into the bowl.

Explain that the student will have a phonogram race. She gets to race whenever the penny bowl is empty.

You will show her a phonogram. If she reads it correctly the first time, she may take out one penny. If she does not read it correctly, she must drop in one penny. When she empties the bowl of pennies, she may race around the track.

A safe place for the child to run
Bowl
Pennies
Basic Phonogram Flash Cards that need more practice. Include additional cards that are easy for the child to read.

Classroom Arcade Race

Designate a "track." Divide the class into teams with 3-5 children on each team. Drop 2-5 pennies into a bowl for each team. Choose one child from each team to show the cards.

Line up the remaining students on each team. Explain that the students will have a phonogram race. They get to race whenever their penny bowl is empty.

A safe place for the children to run
1 bowl per team
Pennies
Basic Phonogram Flash Cards that need more practice. Include additional cards that are easy for the children to read.

Have the student show the first person in line a phonogram. If she reads it correctly the first time, she may take out one penny and move to the back of the line. If she does not read it correctly, she must drop in one penny and move to the back of the line. The next student then reads the next phonogram… The student who removes the last penny from the bowl races around the track. She then trades places with the student showing the cards to the group.

Spelling Rule

A, E, O, U Usually Say Their Long Sounds at the End of a Syllable

Using Phonogram Game Tiles, write the word *wet.*

w	e	t

Let's read this word together. */w-ĕ-t/ wet*

What happens if I take off the last sound /t/?

w	e

Listen to me read this new word. */w-ē/ we*

What did the vowel say? */ē/*

Is the E saying its long or short vowel sound? *long*

w	e	t

What does it say like this? *wet*

Point to the E.

What sound does this say in *wet*? */ĕ/*

Is /ĕ/ a long or a short sound? *short*

w	e

What does this say? *we*

This is interesting. Let's see if this happens with other words.

Using Phonogram Game Tiles, write the word *met.*

m	e	t

Let's read this word together. */m-ĕ-t/ met*

What happens if I take off the last sound /t/?

m	c

Listen to me read this new word. */m-ē/ me*

What did the vowel say? */ē/*

Is that a long or a short sound? *long*

m	e	t

What does it say like this? *met*

Point to the E.

What sound does this say in *met*? */ĕ/*

Is /ĕ/ a long or a short sound? *short*

m	e

Phonogram Game Tiles

Whiteboard

Red & black dry erase markers

What does this say? *me*

This is interesting. Do you think other vowels do this?

Using Phonogram Game Tiles, write the word *got*.

g	o	t

Let's read this word together. */g-ŏ-t/ got*

What happens if I take off the last sound /t/?

g	o

You try to read it. */g-ō/ go*

What did the vowel say? */ō/*

Is that a long or a short sound? *long*

g	o	t

What does it say like this? *got*

Point to the O.

What sound does this say in *got*? */ŏ/*

Is /ŏ/ a long or a short sound? *short*

g	o

What does this say? *go*

Using Phonogram Game Tiles, write the word *not*.

n	o	t

Let's read this word together. */n-ŏ-t/ not*

What happens if I take off the last sound /t/?

n	o

You try to read it. */n-ō/ no*

Describe what you hear happening in these words. *When the vowel is at the end of the syllable/word it says its long sound.*

The words today had a vowel saying its long sound at the end of the word, but this also happens at the end of the syl-lable in the middle of the word. I will write an example on the board. You do not need to remember this yet, but I want you to see how it works.

Write *open* on the board. Write the O in red and the rest of the word in black.

This says *open.*

Let's count the syllables by putting our hand under our chin. */o-pen/ two syllables*
Do you hear the O saying its long sound at the end of a syllable? *yes*

This leads to our new spelling rule: A E O U usually say their long sounds at the end of the syllable.

Say it with me. *A E O U usually say their long sounds at the end of the syllable.*
Let's march around the room as we say the rule. *A E O U usually say their long sounds at the end of the syllable.*
Let's whisper the rule as we tiptoe around the room. *A E O U usually say their long sounds at the end of the syllable.*

Handwriting

Writing Uppercase F

43.2 Uppercase F – page 12

Compare and contrast the upper- and lowercase /f/ in a bookface font and in the handwriting font.

Whiteboard

Tactile Card ℱ or E

For cursive only: ℱ

Cursive Only

Show the Tactile Card ℱ.
What does this say? */t/*

Show the Tactile Card ℱ.
What does this say? */f/*

What do you notice is the same between uppercase /t/ and uppercase /f/? *They are shaped the same, but /f/ has a cross at the midline.*

Why do you think /f/ has a cross at the midline? *Because when we write it in books it has a cross on the midline.*

Let's learn how to write the uppercase /f/.

Demonstrate how to write /f/ using ℱ or E .

Start just below the top line.
①**Slash** down to the baseline, ②**scoop** up to halfway between the baseline and the midline, ③**glide** across, ④pick up the pencil, ⑤**swerve** at the top, ⑥pick up the pencil, ⑦**cross** at the midline.

Start at the top line. ①**Straight** to the baseline, ②pick up the pencil ③**cross** at the top line, ④pick up the pencil, ⑤**cross** at the midline.

Write uppercase /f/ three times on the Tactile Card or in the air, using your pointer finger.

Write uppercase /f/ three times on your whiteboard.
Which one sits on the baseline the best?
Which one has the cross right on the midline?
Which one looks most like the Tactile Card?
Put a smiley face next to the best /f/.

Writing on Paper

43.2 Uppercase F – page 12

Write uppercase /f/ three times on your favorite line size.

Spelling

Spelling List

Teach the words using the steps for Spelling Analysis. Direct students to write the words on their whiteboards or with Phonogram Game Tiles.

Multi-Sensory Fun

Write the words in shaving cream!

	Word	Sentence	Say to Spell	Markings	Spelling Hints
1.	he	*He is at the store.*	hē	hē	Draw a line over the /ē/. A E O U usually say their long sounds at the end of the syllable.
2.	she	*She is my friend.*	shē	s̲h̲ē	Underline /sh/. Draw a line over the /ē/. A E O U usually say their long sounds at the end of the syllable.
3.	go	*He will go with us.*	gō	gō	Draw a line over the /ō/. A E O U usually say their long sounds at the end of the syllable.
4.	so	*He has so much candy.*	sō	sō	Draw a line over the /ō/. A E O U usually say their long sounds at the end of the syllable.
5.	drop	*Do not drop the glass.*	drŏp	drop	All first sounds.

he

The first word is *he*. He is at the store. *he*
Before we write it, segment the word aloud. */h-ē/*
Now write *he* on your whiteboard. As you write it, say each of the sounds aloud. */h-ē/*
The student writes *he* on her whiteboard.

It is now my turn to write *he*. Drive my marker by sounding it out. */h-ē/*
The teacher writes the word on the board.

Why did the E say its long sound /ē/? *A E O U usually say their long sounds at the end of a syllable.*
Let's read it together. */h-ē/ he*

she

The second word is *she*. She is my friend. *she*
Before we write it, segment the word aloud. */sh-ē/*
Write each of the sounds on your whiteboard as you hear them. As you write it, say each of the sounds aloud. */sh-ē/*

The student writes *she* on her whiteboard.

It is now my turn to write *she*. Drive my marker by sounding it out. */sh-ē/*

The teacher writes the word on the board.

Do you see two letters working together to say one sound? */sh/*
Underline /sh/.
Why did the E say its long sound /ē/? *A E O U usually say their long sounds at the end of the syllable.*
Let's read it together. */sh-ē/ she*

go

The third word is *go*. He will go with us. *go*
Before we write it, segment the word aloud. */g-ō/*
Now write each of the sounds on your whiteboard as you hear them. As you write it, say each of the sounds aloud. */g-ō/*

The student writes *go* on her whiteboard.

It is now my turn to write *go*. Drive my marker by sounding it out. */g-ō/*

The student sounds out */g-ō/* while the teacher writes the word on the board.

Why did the O say its long sound /ō/? *A E O U usually say their long sounds at the end of a syllable.*
Let's read it together. */g-ō/ go*

Reading

Word Bingo

43.3 Word Bingo – pages 13-14

Bingo game pieces such as pennies, raisins, or other small tokens

Using the Bingo game provided in the workbook, call out words while the students cover them. Play until the board is covered. Ask the students to read the words as they uncover each square on the board.

Objectives

PHONEMIC AWARENESS: Review syllables.

RULE: Sentences begin with an uppercase letter and end with an end mark.

HANDWRITING: Learn uppercase H .

SPELLING: we, is, thin, had, did

Materials

NEEDED: LOE whiteboard, Basic Phonogram Flash Cards, Tactile Card H or H , Phonogram Chart, a children's book, crayons or markers

OPTIONAL: Phonogram Game Tiles, drum, masking tape or balance beam, paper for a poster, scissors

Phonemic Awareness

Syllables

Today we will practice syllables by marching.

I will say a word. Place your hand under your chin, say the word, count the syllables. Then we will say the word again broken into syllables and march to each syllable.

> **Multi-Sensory Fun**
>
> Provide students with a drum to pound with each syllable.

sandbox *sandbox, two*
Student marches two steps while saying *sand box.*

bookshelf *bookshelf, two*
Student marches two steps while saying *book shelf.*

fish *fish, one*
Student marches one step while saying *fish.*

mailman *mailman, two*
Student marches two steps while saying *mail man.*

kangaroo *kangaroo, three*
Student marches three steps while saying *kang a roo.*

umbrella *umbrella, three*
Student marches three steps while saying *um brel la.*

cat *cat, one*
Student marches one step while saying *cat.*

computer *computer, three*
Student marches three steps while saying *com pu ter.*

ABC Song

Sing the ABC song as we point to each of the phonograms.

Phonogram Chart

Phonogram Practice

Phonogram Tight Rope

Direct the student to stand against the wall. Show her a phonogram. Ask her to read the sounds. If she reads it correctly, she may take one step forward. Her heel must touch her toe for each step. Then she should write the phonogram in the air. If she writes it correctly she may take another step. When she reaches (choose a location) she wins the game.

Basic Phonogram Flash Cards learned so far

Multi-Sensory Fun

Make a line on the floor with masking tape, or use a balance beam.

Classroom: Phonogram Stop and Go

Choose one student to be the "Stop and Go Light." This student will hold a set of all the Phonogram Cards that have been learned so far. Line up the remaining students side by side in a line facing the "Stop and Go Light."

Basic Phonogram Flash Cards learned so far

When the student with the Phonogram Cards turns his back to the students, they must remain still. The "Stop and Go Light" announces how the students will move forward. For example: tiptoe, baby steps, giant steps… The "Stop and Go Light" turns around showing a phonogram. The students read all the sounds. For each sound, they can take one step forward. The "Stop and Go Light" turns back around, chooses the next phonogram, and announces how they will move forward. When the students reach the "Stop and Go Light," a new student is chosen to lead.

Handwriting

Writing Uppercase H

44.1 Uppercase H – page 15

Compare and contrast the upper- and lowercase /h/ in a bookface font and in the handwriting font.

Let's learn how to write the uppercase /h/.

Demonstrate how to write /h/ using ⬚ or ⬚ .

Whiteboard
Tactile Card ⬚ or ⬚

Start halfway between the mid-line and the top line. ①**Curve** up to the top line, ②**straight** to the baseline, ③pick up the pencil, start at the top line, ④**straight** to the baseline, ⑤slide **up** to the midline, ⑥**swirl**.

Start at the top line. ①**Straight** to the baseline, ②pick up the pencil, start at the top line, ③**straight** to the baseline, ④pick up the pencil, ⑤**cross** at the midline.

Write uppercase /h/ three times on the Tactile Card or in the air, using your pointer finger.

Write uppercase /h/ three times on your whiteboard.
Which one sits on the baseline the best?
Which one looks most like the Tactile Card?
Put a smiley face next to the best /h/.

Writing on Paper

44.1 Uppercase H – page 15

Write uppercase /h/ three times on your favorite line size.

When do you think we use a question mark? *for a question*

We use an exclamation point to show someone has a strong feeling.

Writers also use uppercase letters to write names. Names are important, so we always start them with an uppercase letter.

Matching

44.2 Matching – pages 16-17

Look at the page. Point to an uppercase letter or a capital letter on the page.

Point to a period.

A sentence begins with a capital (uppercase) letter, ends with an end mark, and tells a complete thought.

Read each sentence and match it to the picture.

Markers or crayons
Scissors

Challenge

Read one of the sentences and ask the student to write it on the whiteboard.

Multi-Sensory Fun

Cut out the sentences and pictures and play a matching game.

Multi-Sensory Fun

Cut out the sentences. Ask a boy and a girl to come to the front of the room. Ask a student to choose a sentence and read it aloud. Either the boy or girl acts it out.

Objectives

PHONEMIC AWARENESS: Learn about schwa as a lazy vowel sound.

HANDWRITING: Learn uppercase M .

SPELLING: a, his, the, then, path

READER 1

Materials

NEEDED: LOE whiteboard, Tactile Card m or M , Phonogram Chart, paper or poster board for a Lazy Vowel Chart, chocolate chips or tokens for Bingo, Reader 1

OPTIONAL: Phonogram Game Tiles, books from book list

Phonogram Practice

Write and Erase

Explain to your student that you will read eight phonogram sounds. The first time she hears the sound, she must write it on her board. The second time she hears the sound she should erase it. Explain that you will not read them all in order, so she must listen carefully and check to see if she has already written it.

Whiteboard

/sh/
Students write "sh."

/z/
Students erase "z."

/y-ĭ-ī-ē/
Students write "y."

/ks/
Students write "x."

/sh/
Students erase "sh."

/th-TH/
Students erase "th."

/z/
Students write "z."

/v/
Students write "v."

/th-TH/
Students write "th."

/y-ĭ-ī-ē/
Students erase "y."

/f/
Students write "f."

/f/
Students erase "f."

/k/
Students write "k."

/v/
Students erase "v."

/k/
Students erase "k."

/ks/
Students erase "x."

Handwriting

Writing Uppercase M

45.1 Uppercase M – page 18

Whiteboard
Tactile Card *m* or *M*

Compare and contrast the upper- and lowercase /m/ in a bookface font and in the handwriting font.

Let's learn how to write the uppercase /m/.

Demonstrate how to write /m/ using *m* or *M* .

Start halfway between the mid-line and the top line. [1]**Curve** up to the top line, [2]**straight** to the baseline, [3]**bump** up to the top line, [4]**straight** to the baseline, [5]**bump** up to the top line, [6]**down**.

Start at the top line. [1]**Straight** to the baseline, [2]pick up the pencil, start at the top line, [3]**kick** down to the midline, [4]**angle up** to the top line, [5]**straight** to the baseline.

Write uppercase /m/ three times on the Tactile Card or in the air, using your pointer finger.

Write uppercase /m/ three times on your whiteboard.
Which one sits on the baseline the best?
Which one looks most like the Tactile Card?
Put a smiley face next to the best /m/.

Writing on Paper

45.1 Uppercase M – page 18

Write uppercase /m/ three times on your favorite line size.

Phonemic Awareness

ABC Song

Sing the ABC song as we point to each of the phonograms.

Schwa: The Special Vowel Sound

Are you ever lazy?

When you are lazy do you want to move around? *no*

Do you try to move as little as possible? *yes*

Today we are going to learn about a special vowel sound in English. It is a lazy vowel sound.

Let's do an experiment. Which sound makes your mouth move more when you say it?

Compare /ā/ and /ə/. */ā/ moves more.*
/ə/ is a lazy sound.

Compare /ē/ and /ə/. */ē/ moves more.*
/ə/ is a lazy sound.

Compare /ă/ and /ə/. */ă/ moves more.*
/ə/ is a lazy sound.

Sometimes, when we hear the sound /ə/, it is a vowel being lazy. We are not opening our mouths big enough to say the vowel clearly. We call this lazy vowel a schwa sound.

Write ə on the board.

Dictionaries write this sound like an upside down E. Schwa is so lazy it doesn't even stand up.

Does the schwa sound /ə/ remind you of a phonogram you know? *Yes, /ŭ-ū-ö-ü/.*

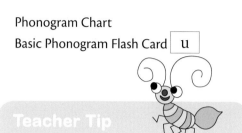

Phonogram Chart
Basic Phonogram Flash Card u

Teacher Tip

Schwa /ə/ usually sounds like /ŭ/ as in *po-lite* or *about*. Occasionally schwa may sound like /ĭ/ as in *trumpet* or *precise*.

Teacher Tip

Technically, schwa is an unstressed vowel sound. In English, syllables and words have varying amounts of stress. When a syllable is unstressed, the vowel is sometimes not clearly articulated. When we add affixes to a word, the stress may shift and the vowel may then be clearly pronounced. For more information see *Uncovering the Logic of English* pages 124-127.

Teacher Tip

A few grammatical words in English such as *the*, *was*, and *from* have a schwa sound in a one-syllable word. This is because these words are not stressed in English sentences. For more information see *Uncovering the Logic of English* pages 124-127.

When we hear the sound /ŭ/ in a word, we need to be careful to find out if it is this phonogram u , or if it is one of our other vowels being lazy and saying /ə/.

When we are learning our spelling words, two of them will have a vowel saying its schwa sound /ə/. Listen for a lazy vowel and raise your hand when you hear it.

Spelling

Spelling List

Teach the words using the steps for Spelling Analysis. Direct students to write the words on their whiteboards or with Phonogram Game Tiles.

Word	Sentence	Say to Spell	Markings	Spelling Hints
1. a	*A cat ran across the road.*	ā	a	See dialog below.
2. his	*That is his coat.*	hĭz	his²	Put a 2 over the /s-z/. It said its second sound /z/.
3. the	*The sweater is itchy.*	THē	<u>th</u>ē²	Underline /TH/. Put a 2 over the /th-TH/. It said its second sound /TH/. Draw a line over the /ē/. A E O U usually say their long sounds at the end of the syllable.
4. then	*After we eat dinner, then we will play a game.*	THĕn	<u>th</u>en²	Underline /TH/. Put a 2 over the /th-TH/. It said its second sound /TH/.
5. path	*Please walk on the path.*	păth	pa<u>th</u>	Underline /th/.

a

The first word is *a*. A cat ran across the road. *a*
Did you hear a schwa sound in *a*? **yes**
This time, it is the phonogram /ă-ā-ä/ being lazy and saying /ə/.
If we said the vowel clearly, it would say /ā/.
Let's sound it out. /ā/
Now write /ā/ on your whiteboard.
The student writes *a* on her whiteboard.

Now help me to write it by sounding it out. /ā/
The teacher writes *a* on the board.

What does the A usually say at the end of the syllable? /ā/
Why? *A E O U usually say their long sounds at the end of the syllable.*
But how do we usually read this word? /ə/

Multi-Sensory Fun

For fun, when students discover a word with a lazy vowel sound, say "You've been schwaed."

his

The next word is *his*. That is his coat. *his*
Before we write it, segment the word aloud. */h-ĭ-z/*
You will use /s-z/ to spell *his*. How will you spell /z/? **with a /s-z/**
Now write each of the sounds on your whiteboard as you hear them. As you write it, say each of the sounds aloud. */h-ĭ-z/*

The student writes *his* on her whiteboard.

It is now my turn to write *his*. Drive my marker by sounding it out. */h-ĭ-z/*

The teacher writes the word on the board.

What sound of /s-z/ do we hear in *his*? */z/*
Is this the first or the second sound? **second**
Since /s-z/ is saying its second sound, we will write a 2 over it to remind us that it is saying its second sound /z/. Let's read it together. */h-ĭ-z/ his*

the

The third word is *the*. The sweater is itchy. *the*
Did you hear a schwa sound in *the*? **yes**
In this case, it is the phonogram /ĕ-ē/ being lazy and saying /ə/. If we said the vowel clearly, it would say /TH-ē/. Let's sound it out. */TH-e/*
Now write /TH-ē/ on your whiteboard.

The student writes *the* on her whiteboard.

Now help me to write it by sounding it out. */TH-ē/*

The teacher writes *the* on the board.

Do you see any multi-letter phonograms we should underline? */TH/*
What sound of /th-TH/ is this? **the second sound**
Since it is saying its second sound, let's write a 2 over it.
What will the E say at the end of the syllable? */ē/*
But how do we usually read this word? */THə/*

Book List

In some lessons, book lists will be provided. Books in these lists have been evaluated for phonograms, spelling rules, uppercase letters, and tricky high frequency words. These books can be read successfully by your student at this point in Foundations without guessing. You may choose any books on these lists for your student to read to himself or aloud.

Book List

Bob Books Set 1
    Mat
    Sam
Explain O.K. as an abbreviation where we read the letter names, not the sounds. Point out the periods.
    Mac

Teacher Tip

Schwa /ə/ usually sounds like /ŭ/ as in p<u>o</u>lite or <u>about</u>. Occasionally schwa may sound like /ĭ/ as in pr<u>e</u>cise.

Phonemic Awareness

Lazy Vowel Words

When we find words with a schwa sound, we will add them
to a Lazy Vowel Chart.

Large piece of paper or poster board

Write "Lazy Vowels," "ə," and "Schwa" at the top of the chart.
Which words did we learn today that have a schwa: a lazy vowel sound? *a, the*
Let's add them to our chart.

How do we say to spell *a*? */ā/*
How do we say to spell *the*? */TH-ē/*
Write it on the chart while sounding out /TH-ē/.
How do we usually pronounce this word? */THə/*

Reading

Reader

Take out Reader 1. Ask the student to read the title and each
page aloud.

Discuss the meaning of Fred's sign on page 2.

When the student has finished the book, ask:
Who does Fred think he is?
What does Fred want to do?
Did you like the story? Why or why not?

In a classroom, ask the students to bring the book home to
read to their parents.

Reader 1

Teacher Tip

Some students have not developed the
visual muscle memory required to focus
on the words when there are images on
the page. If the student is struggling to
read the words, cover the pictures with a
blank piece of paper.

Word Bingo

45.2 Word Bingo – pages 19-20

Chocolate chips or other small tokens
to cover the Bingo squares

Play Bingo using the game board provided in the workbook.
Call out a word for the students to put a token on. Play until
the board is covered. Ask the student to read the words as he removes each token.

REVIEW A

Area	Skill	Mastery
Phonemic Awareness	Distinguish short and long vowel sounds.	2
	Count and divide syllables.	3
	Recognize the schwa sound.	3
Handwriting	Write lowercase a-z.	1
	Write uppercase S, T, F, H, M.*	2
Phonograms & Spelling Rules	Read lowercase a-z.	1
	Read the uppercase letters S, T, F, H, M.*	2
	Read sh, th.	2
	Know that schwa is a lazy vowel sound.	3
Reading	Read CVC words.	1
	Read one-syllable words ending in a long vowel.	2
	Read the high frequency words: this, that, he, she, go, so, we, is, had, a, his, the.	2

The goal is to develop familiarity with the uppercase letters. Students should be able to read the sounds; however, many students will need to refer to a handwriting chart for more than a year when writing them. This is because they are not used frequently in students' writing at this stage.

The chart on the previous page lists the literacy skills that have been introduced in the first five lessons. Skills with a 1 should be mastered before students move on to the next lesson. For skills marked with a 2, students should demonstrate familiarity but not necessarily answer all the questions correctly. These skills will be practiced extensively in the upcoming lessons. Skills with a 3 do not need to be mastered in order for students to move on. Some level 3 skills will be covered extensively in later lessons. Others are not necessary for becoming strong readers and spellers, but they have proved beneficial for some students. Level 3 skills are listed in the chart, but they are not included in the assessments.

Phonemic Awareness Assessment

Short and Long Vowels

A.1 Long and Short Vowels – page 21

I will read a vowel sound. Put your finger on it. Then follow my instruction.

/ă/, short /ă/. Circle short /ă/.
/ū/, long /ū/. Underline long /ū/.
/ŏ/, short /ŏ/. Put an X on short /ŏ/.

Teacher Tip

Alternatively, ask the student to read each of the sounds.

Handwriting Assessment

Handwriting

A.2 Handwriting – page 22

Write one of each phonogram on your favorite line size.

Multi-Sensory Fun

If the student is not ready to write on paper, show the student the phonogram card and have him write the phonogram on a whiteboard or in a sensory box.

Phonogram Assessment

Phonogram Assessment

Ask the student to read each of the following phonogram cards: v, x, y, z, sh, th

Basic Phonogram Flash Cards

| v | x | y | z | sh | th |

What's That Phonogram?

A.3 What's That Phonogram? – page 23

On your page are groups of four phonograms. I will say a phonogram's sound(s). Color the phonogram with your highlighter.

Highlighter

1. /sh/
2. /th-TH/
3. /v/
4. /ks/
5. /y-ĭ-ī-ē/

Reading Assessment

Reading

A.4 Reading – page 24

Cover up the pictures on the right with a blank sheet of paper. Ask the student to read the first sentence aloud. Uncover the pictures. Ask the student to point to the picture that matches. Cover the pictures again. Read the second sentence…

High Frequency Words

A.5 High Frequency Words – page 25

At this point, students should be beginning to develop strategies to read each of these words. If the student reads eight or more of the words correctly by sounding them out, move on to lessons 46-50. We will continue to work on fluency extensively in the upcoming lessons.

Read each word. If you read it correctly the first time, you may add a block to the tower. When you have completed the list, you may knock down the tower.

Teacher Tip

Students should be able to sound out the words at this point and comprehend each sentence. If the student stumbles, point to the sound that he is missing and ask him to re-read the word. This is not a fluency test. The goal is for the child to have a way to approach each word phonetically. Fluency will be worked on extensively in later lessons.

LEGO®s or blocks

Teacher Tip

For students struggling with visual distraction, cover the words that are not being read with a blank piece of paper.

Phonogram Practice

Phonogram Flip

46.1 Phonogram Flip – page 27

Scissors

Cut along the green dotted lines to create flaps. Stop at
the solid red line. Fold the page in half along the solid
red line. Ask the student to choose a flap, read the phonogram, then open the flap and write the phonogram on the line.

Optional Blind Writing

Whiteboard

Call out the phonogram sound(s) and ask the students to
write them on their whiteboard with their eyes closed.
Blind writing is a great way to aid students in developing muscle memory for handwriting.
Use the activity to emphasize the rhythm and motions.

Phonemic Awareness

Creating New Words

Today we will make new words using phonogram tiles.
I have arranged the letters in a pattern. Read the word I have
created.

Phonogram Game Tiles for A-Z and ck

i	ck

What does this say? *ick*

What happens if I add /s/ to the beginning of *ick*?

s	i	ck

What does this say? *sick*

If I take off the /s/ and replace it with /l/, I can form a new word.

l	i	ck

What does this say? *lick*

What do I get if I add /s/ to the beginning?

s	l	i	ck

What does this say? *slick*

What do we get if we change the /sl/ like this?

t	r	i	ck

What does this say? *trick*

What do we get if we change the /t/ to a /b/?

| b | r | i | ck |

What does this say? *brick*

Now we will change the vowel.

| a | ck |

What does this say? */ăck/*

Is /ăck/ a word? *no*

What letter or letters could you add to the beginning of /ăck/ to make a word?

Allow students to create words as long as they are attentive. Some possible words are:

back	quack	snack
black	rack	tack
jack	sack	track
lack	slack	
pack	smack	

ABC Song

Sing the ABC song as we point to each of the phonograms.

Phonogram Chart

Handwriting

Writing Uppercase N

Whiteboard

Tactile Card 𝓃 or 𝒩

46.2 Uppercase N – page 29

Compare and contrast the upper- and lowercase /n/ in a bookface font and in the handwriting font.

Let's learn how to write the uppercase /n/.

Demonstrate how to write /n/ using 𝓃 or 𝒩 .

Start halfway between the mid-line and the top line. ①**Curve** up to the top line, ②**straight** to the baseline, ③**bump** up to the top line, ④**down**.

Start at the top line. ①**Straight** to the baseline, ②pick up the pencil, start at the top line, ③**kick** down to the baseline, ④**straight up** to the top line.

Objectives

PHONEMIC AWARENESS: Create new words by changing the first sound.

SPELLING RULE: Two-letter /k/ is used only after a single, short vowel.

HANDWRITING: Learn uppercase A .

SPELLING: be, me, shut, rock, shot

Materials

NEEDED: LOE whiteboard, Basic Phonogram Flash Cards ck and phonograms learned so far, stop watch, Tactile Card a or A , Phonogram Chart

OPTIONAL: Phonogram Game Tiles, scissors

Phonogram Practice

Phonogram Reading Race

Today you will race yourself. I will show you a phonogram. Read the sounds. When you have read all of these phonograms, I will stop the stopwatch. Then we will try again and see if you can beat your time.

Basic Phonogram Flash Cards learned so far

Stop watch

Phonemic Awareness

ABC Song

Sing the ABC song as we point to each of the phonograms.

Phonogram Chart

47.1 Vowels – page 31

On this page is a list of vowels with short and long markings. Read the green vowels to me. *ă ĕ ĭ ŏ ŭ*
Read the blue vowels to me. *ā ē ī ō ŭ*
What color are the short sounds? *green*
What color are the long sounds? *blue*

47.2 The Phonogram CK – page 32

Look at each of the pictures on the page. Find the phonogram(s) needed to complete the word. Write it in the blank.

Spelling Rule

The Phonogram CK

47.2 The Phonogram CK – page 32

Now I have a mystery for you to solve. You will be a word detective and discover when we use two-letter /k/. First, read each of the words aloud and underline two-letter /k/.

Basic Phonogram Flash Card | ck |

Now read the words again. This time listen for whether the vowel is short or long. Mark the vowel sound. Remember, we put a curved line over a short sound and a straight line over a long sound.

lock short
brick short ...

What kind of vowel sound do you hear before a two-letter /k/? *They are all short sounds.*
Is two-letter /k/ always after a short vowel? *yes*
Is two-letter /k/ ever after a long vowel? *no*
This leads us to a spelling rule. Two letter /k/ is used only after a single, short vowel.

Let's whisper the rule together. *Two letter /k/ is used only after a single, short vowel.*
Let's sing the rule. *Two letter /k/ is used only after a single, short vowel.*
Let's shout the rule. *Two letter /k/ is used only after a single, short vowel.*

When you are reading and you see a two-letter /k/, you will know that the vowel sound is short.

Handwriting

Writing Uppercase A

47.3 Uppercase A – page 33

Whiteboard
Tactile Card a or A

Compare and contrast the upper- and lowercase /ă-ā-ä/ in a bookface font and in the handwriting font.

Let's learn how to write the uppercase /ă-ā-ä/.

Demonstrate how to write /ă-ā-ä/ using a or A .

Start at the top line. [①]**Roll** around to the baseline, [②]**swing** up to the top line, [③]**down** to the baseline.

Start at the top line. [①]**Slash** down to the baseline, [②]pick up the pencil, start at the top line, [③]**kick** down to the baseline, [④]pick up the pencil, [⑤]**cross** at the midline.

Write uppercase /ă-ā-ä/ three times on the Tactile Card or in the air, using your pointer finger.

Write uppercase /ă-ā-ä/ three times on your whiteboard.
Which one sits on the baseline the best?
Which one looks most like the Tactile Card?
Put a smiley face next to the best /ă-ā-ä/.

Writing on Paper

47.3 Uppercase A – page 33

Write uppercase /ă-ā-ä/ three times on your favorite line size.

Upper- and Lowercase Letters

47.4 Matching Phonograms – page 34

Draw a line to match the uppercase and lowercase letters on your page.

Spelling

Spelling List

Teach the words using the steps for Spelling Analysis. Direct students to write the words on their whiteboards or with Phonogram Game Tiles.

	Word	Sentence	Say to Spell	Markings	Spelling Hints
1.	be	*Please be quiet.*	bē	bē	Draw a line over the /ē/. A E O U usually say their long sounds at the end of the syllable.
2.	me	*He gave me a book.*	mē	mē	Draw a line over the /ē/. A E O U usually say their long sounds at the end of the syllable.
3.	shut	*Shut the door, please.*	shŭt	s̲h̲ut	Underline /sh/.
4.	rock	*I tripped on a rock.*	rŏk	ro̲c̲k̲	Underline two-letter /k/. Used only after a single, short vowel.
5.	shot	*He made a perfect shot!*	shŏt	s̲h̲ot	Underline /sh/.

Teacher Tip

Ask the students to recite the rule "A E O U usually say their long sounds at the end of the syllable" in different voices (loud, soft, silly, singing) after teaching *be* and *me*.

There are only six one-syllable words that use a single-letter E to say the long /ē/ sound at the end of the word. These are: *he, she, we, me, be, the*. These have now all been introduced.

Reading

Matching

47.5 Matching – pages 35-36

Read the sentence. Match it to the correct picture.

Multi-Sensory Fun

Cut out the sentences and pictures. Hide the sentences throughout the room. Show the child the pictures. Ask the child to find a sentence, read it aloud, then match it to the correct picture.

Objectives

PHONEMIC AWARENESS: Practice blending.

PHONOGRAM: Learn igh .

HANDWRITING: Learn uppercase D .

SPELLING: black, light, night, wish, snack

Materials

NEEDED: LOE whiteboard, Basic Phonogram Flash Card igh , Tactile Card 𝒟 or 𝒟 , large whiteboard, NERF® gun or small soft ball, small crackers or treats, Phonogram Chart, scissors

OPTIONAL: Sensory box, Phonogram Game Tiles, books from book list

Phonograms

The Phonogram igh

Show the Phonogram Card igh .

This says /ī/. What does it say? */ī/*
I like to call this three-letter /ī/. Why do you think I call it three-letter /ī/? *It says /ī/ and it has three letters.*
Write three-letter /ī/ three times on your whiteboard.

Whiteboard
Basic Phonogram Flash Card igh

Phonogram Practice

Phonogram Target

Say a phonogram's sound(s). Direct the student to write the phonogram someplace on a large whiteboard to create a target. When all the phonograms have been written, tell the student to step back 3-5 steps. Explain that you will now read a phonogram, and she should hit the phonogram by throwing the ball at it, or by shooting it with the NERF® gun.

Large whiteboard
Small, soft ball
NERF® gun with suction cup darts

Handwriting

Writing Uppercase D

48.1 Uppercase D – page 37

Compare and contrast the upper- and lowercase /d/ in a bookface font and in the handwriting font.

Let's learn how to write the uppercase /d/.

Demonstrate how to write /d/ using or 𝒟 .

Whiteboard
Tactile Card 𝒟 or 𝒟

 *Start just below the top line.* ①**Slash** down past the midline, ②**loop** on the baseline, ③**roll** to the topline, ④**swirl**.

Start at the top line. ①**Straight** to the baseline, ② slide **up** to the top line, ③**circle** around to the baseline, ④touch.

Write uppercase /d/ three times on the Tactile Card or in the air, using your pointer finger.

Write uppercase /d/ three times on your whiteboard.
Which one looks most like the Tactile Card?
Put a smiley face next to the best /d/.

Writing on Paper

48.1 Uppercase D – page 37

Write uppercase /d/ three times on your favorite line size.

Phonemic Awareness

Blending Practice

48.2 Blends – page 38

Today we will practice blending two and three sounds. These sounds do not make words. I want to see if you can say the sounds these phonograms make when they are put next to each other. On your worksheet are a series of letters in boxes. Each time you read one of them correctly, you may put a treat on the square. When you have read them all, then you may enjoy the treats.

ABC Song

Sing the ABC song as we point to each of the phonograms.

Crackers or other small treats

Sensory box

Teacher Tip

Be aware of the student's energy. It is not necessary for him to read all the blends on the page.

Challenge

Say a blend. Ask the student to write the phonograms that make up the sound on a whiteboard or in a sensory box.

Phonogram Chart

Spelling

Spelling List

Teach the words for students to write on their whiteboards. Use the steps for Spelling Analysis.

	Word	Sentence	Say to Spell	Markings	Spelling Hints
1.	black	*Wear your black pants to the concert.*	blăk	bla<u>ck</u>	Underline two-letter /k/. CK is used only after a single, short vowel.
2.	light	*We need to turn on the light.*	līt	li<u>gh</u>t	Underline three-letter /ī/.
3.	night	*It is dark at night.*	nīt	ni<u>gh</u>t	Underline three-letter /ī/.
4.	wish	*Make a wish.*	wĭsh	wi<u>sh</u>	Underline /sh/.
5.	snack	*He ate a snack.*	snăk	sna<u>ck</u>	Underline two-letter /k/. Used only after a single, short vowel.

Reading

High Frequency Word Practice

48.3 High Frequency Word Game – page 39

Scissors

Cut out the words. Divide them equally among three, six, or nine stations around the room. Designate a starting line. Tell the student he is to run to the first station, read the words aloud, then run to the next station, read the words, etc. until he has read the words at all the stations.

High Frequency Word Practice Classroom

48.3 High Frequency Word Game – page 39

Scissors

Cut out the words. Divide them equally among three, six, or nine stations around the room. Assign one student per station to listen to other students read the words. Designate a starting line. Tell the first student he is to run to the first station, read the words aloud, then run to the next station, read the words, etc. until he has read the words at all the stations. When the first student has completed the first station, the second student may go.

Teacher Tip

Before beginning, be sure that each of the checkers can read each of the words at his station. Explain that if a student misses a word, he is not to just tell them the answer, but rather should help the student to sound it out. If a student is having particular difficulty with a word, have him be the checker at the station for extra practice.

Teacher Tip

Laminate the High Frequency Word Cards and save them for use with other High Frequency Word Games.

Book List

Bob Books Set 1
　　Dot
　　Dot and Mit
　　Dot and the Dog

Objectives

PHONEMIC AWARENESS: Practice blending.

PHONOGRAM: Learn ch .

HANDWRITING: Learn uppercase B .

SPELLING: chin, chick, no, bright, bath

Materials

NEEDED: LOE whiteboard, Phonogram Chart, all the Basic Phonogram Flash Cards learned so far and ch , Tactile Card B or B , three bases and a home plate, scissors, markers or crayons

OPTIONAL: Highlighter, Phonogram Game Tiles

Handwriting

Writing Uppercase B

49.1 Uppercase B – page 41

Compare and contrast the upper- and lowercase /b/ in a bookface font and in the handwriting font.

Let's learn how to write the uppercase /b/.

Demonstrate how to write uppercase /b/ using B or B .

Whiteboard
Tactile Card B or B

52

Start halfway between the midline and the top line. ①**Curve** up to the top line, ②**straight** to the baseline, ③**slide up** to the top line, ④**circle** around to the midline, ⑤**circle** around past the baseline, ⑥touch, ⑦**glide** across.

 Start at the top line. ①**Straight** to the baseline, ②slide **up** to the top line, ③**circle** around to the midline, ④touch, ⑤**circle** around to the baseline, ⑥touch.

Write uppercase /b/ three times on the Tactile Card or in the air, using your pointer finger.

Write uppercase /b/ three times on your whiteboard.
Which one sits on the baseline the best?
Which one looks most like the Tactile Card?
Put a smiley face next to the best /b/.

Writing on Paper

49.1 Uppercase B – page 41

Write uppercase /b/ three times on your favorite line size.

Phonemic Awareness

ABC Song

Let's sing the ABC song as we point to each of the phonograms.

Phonogram Chart

49.2 Blending – pages 43-44

Cut along the green dotted lines to create flaps. Stop at the solid red line. Fold the page in half along the solid red line. Read the blend on the flap, then open the flap and read the word underneath.

Scissors
Highlighter

Multi-Sensory Fun

Highlight the blend in the word.

Phonograms

The Phonogram ch

Show the Phonogram Card ch .

> This says /ch-k-sh/.
> What does it say? */ch-k-sh/*
> How many sounds is that? *three*

Whiteboard
Basic Phonogram Flash Card ch

Move your arms in a train motion as you say the sounds.

> This phonogram reminds me of a train. Let's march around the room saying /ch-k-sh/.
> Write /ch-k-sh/ three times on your whiteboard.

Phonogram Practice

Phonogram Baseball

Choose the location for home plate and each of the three bases. The student "up to bat" stands on home plate with a whiteboard and dry erase marker. The teacher chooses a phonogram card and reads it to the batter. The batter writes the phonogram on her whiteboard. If it is spelled correctly, she advances to the next base. If it is not spelled correctly, she is "out" and must move back to the home plate. At each base, she is given another phonogram to spell. Each time she crosses home plate, she is awarded 1 point.

Basic Phonogram Flash Cards
Whiteboard
3 bases and a home plate

Phonogram Baseball for the Classroom

Choose the location for home plate and each of the three bases. Divide the class into two teams. The student "up to bat" stands on home plate with a whiteboard and dry erase marker. The "pitcher" chooses a phonogram card and reads it to the batter. The batter writes the phonogram on her whiteboard. If it is spelled correctly, she advances to the next base. If it is not spelled correctly, she is "out." The next "batter" then moves into position with her whiteboard. The "pitcher" reads a new phonogram. The batter must write it on her whiteboard correctly to advance. Likewise each player on base must write it correctly to advance. Anyone who misspells the phonogram is "out." Each time a player crosses home plate, her team is awarded 1 point. Three outs and the team is out, and play advances to the next team.

Basic Phonogram Flash Cards
4 whiteboards
3 bases and a home plate

Optional: Assign "basemen" to check the spelling at each base.

Spelling

Spelling List

Teach the words using the steps for Spelling Analysis. Direct students to write the words on their whiteboards or with Phonogram Game Tiles.

Teacher Tip

Remember to use finger spelling while students segment the word to cue when to use a multi-letter phonogram. For example, hold up one finger for B, one finger for R, three for IGH, and one for T.

	Word	Sentence	Say to Spell	Markings	Spelling Hints
1.	chin	*I scraped my chin.*	chĭn	<u>ch</u>in	Underline /ch/.
2.	chick	*May I hold the baby chick?*	chĭk	<u>ch</u>i<u>ck</u>	Underline /ch/. Underline two-letter /k/. Used only after a single, short vowel.
3.	no	*No, that is not the answer.*	nō	nō	Draw a line over the /ō/. A E O U usually say their long sounds at the end of the syllable.
4.	bright	*The light is very bright.*	brīt	br<u>igh</u>t	Underline three-letter /ī/.
5.	bath	*It is time for your bath.*	băth	ba<u>th</u>	Underline /th/.

Reading

The Duck's Snack

49.3 The Duck's Snack – pages 45-46

Read the story aloud. Then go back and read each sentence. Draw a picture in each box. Read the story to someone and share the illustrations you drew.

Markers or crayons

Objectives

PHONEMIC AWARENESS: Review short and long vowels.

PHONOGRAM: Learn ee .

HANDWRITING: Learn uppercase P .

SPELLING: three, back, see, feel, thick

READER 2

Materials

NEEDED: LOE whiteboard, Basic Phonogram Flash Cards learned so far and ee , Phonogram Chart, Tactile Card *P* or *P* , Reader 2

OPTIONAL: Phonogram Game Tiles

Phonograms

The Phonogram ee

Show the Phonogram Card ee .

> This says /ē/. What does it say? **/ē/**
> I like to call it /ē/ double /ē/, which always says /ē/. Why do
> you think I would call it /ē/ double /ē/, which always says /ē/? **There are two E's and it always says one sound, /ē/.**
> Write /ē/ double /ē/, which always says /ē/, three times on your whiteboard.

Whiteboard
Basic Phonogram Flash Card ee

Phonogram Practice

Phonogram Jump

Direct the student to stand at the opposite end of the room from you. Explain you will show her a phonogram

Basic Phonogram Flash Cards for all phonograms learned so far card. She may take one jump forward as she reads each sound. When she reaches you, she will then take one jump backwards for each sound.

Phonemic Awareness

Short and Long Vowels

I will write a vowel. Read the short sound.

Write *a*.

/ă/

How do we mark the short sound? *with a curved line (breve)*

Draw a breve over the *ă*.

Write o.

/ŏ/

How do we mark the short sound? *with a curved line (breve)*

Draw a breve over the ŏ.

Write e.

/ĕ/

How do we mark the short sound? *with a curved line (breve)*
Draw a breve over the ĕ.

Write uppercase A.

/ă/

How do we mark the short sound? *with a curved line (breve)*
Draw a breve over the Ă.

Write u.

/ŭ/

How do we mark the short sound? *with a curved line (breve)*
Draw a breve over the ŭ.

Now when I write a vowel, read the long sound.

Write u.

/ū/

How do we mark the long sound? *with a straight line*
Draw a straight line over the ū.

Multi-Sensory Fun

Have the students act out the breve and straight line with their arms as they read the sounds.

Challenge

Ask the student to write the vowel and to mark it as long or short.

Spelling

Spelling List

Teach the words using the steps for Spelling Analysis. Direct students to write the words on their whiteboards or with Phonogram Game Tiles.

	Word	Sentence	Say to Spell	Markings	Spelling Hints
1.	three	*Three kids ran across the park.*	thrē	<u>three</u>	Underline /th/. Underline E double E, which always says /ē/.
2.	back	*The back of your coat is muddy.*	băk	ba<u>ck</u>	Underline two-letter /ck/ used only after a single, short vowel.
3.	see	*I see a large tree.*	sē	s<u>ee</u>	Underline E double E, which always says /ē/.
4.	feel	*Feel this soft blanket.*	fēl	f<u>ee</u>l	Underline E double E, which always says /ē/.
5.	thick	*Wear your thick, warm sweater.*	thĭk	<u>thick</u>	Underline /th/. Underline two-letter /k/. Used only after a single, short vowel.

back

The second word is *back*. The back of your coat is muddy. *back*

Place your hand under your chin and say, "back." How many syllables in *back*? **one**

Let's sound it out. */b-ă-k/*

Hmm. What kind of /k/ will I use? **two-letter /k/**

Why? */ă/ is a short vowel.*

Now write /b-ă-k/ on your whiteboard.
The student writes *back* on his whiteboard.

It is now my turn to write *back*. Sound it out as I write it. */b-ă-k/*
The teacher writes *back* on the board.

What does this say? */b-ă-k/ back*

Why did I use two-letter /k/? **Because there is a short vowel.**

How many letters did I use to write /ă/? **one**

Vocabulary

Discuss the meanings of *back*.

My *back* is itchy.
I sit in the *back* seat.
The shed is in the *back* of the house.
Put it *back* where it belongs.

Teacher Tip

Learning to recognize mutiple meanings of words is a vital part of vocabulary development. Ask students to think of sentences that represent various meanings of the same word.

Reading

Reader

Take out Reader 2. Ask the student to read the title and each page aloud.

When the student has finished the book, ask:

What does Max need? *lunch*

How do you think Max is feeling at the beginning of the book? *hungry*

What does Max want for lunch first? *a duck*

What happens? *The duck runs away.*

What does Max have for lunch? *greens*

Ask the student to read the book again later to a parent, sibling, grandparent, or other member of the family.

Reader 2

Multi-Sensory Fun

Some students have not developed the visual muscle memory required to focus on the words on a page when there are images on the page. If the student is struggling to read the words, cover the pictures with a blank piece of paper. Explain that he can look at the picture after he has read the words.

Teacher Tip

Encourage students to sound each word out and see if it makes sense before declaring their answer.

Reading

Reading

B.4 Reading – page 53

Ask the students to read the sentences in their workbook. Note which phonograms or rules cause them to stumble.

If the student reads the sentence smoothly, rate it a 1.

If the student makes 2-3 mistakes or corrects most of the mistakes, rate it a 2.

If the student reads more than half the words incorrectly, rate it a 3.

Short Vowel Sounds

These should be relatively simple for the students to read.

_____ Mom has a cat.

_____ The pan is hot.

_____ Frogs jump.

_____ Drink the milk.

The Phonograms sh th ck igh ch ee

Note which phonograms the student misses.

_____ The black sheep sleep at night.

_____ The chicks peck at the seeds.

_____ She needs a bath.

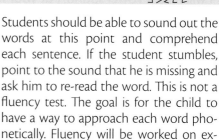

Teacher Tip

Students should be able to sound out the words at this point and comprehend each sentence. If the student stumbles, point to the sound that he is missing and ask him to re-read the word. This is not a fluency test. The goal is for the child to have a way to approach each word phonetically. Fluency will be worked on extensively in later lessons.

Teacher Tip

If the student misreads a multi-letter phonogram, underline it and ask the student to try it again.

Practice Ideas

Short and Long Vowels

Review by showing the phonogram cards a, e, i, o, and u and discussing how the first sound is called the short sound and the second sound is called the long sound.

"Short Vowels" on page 2 of the Teacher's Manual
"Vowels: Sounds You Can Sing" on page 1
"Vowels" on page 4
"Short and Long Vowels" on page 57

Handwriting

Using the Tactile Cards, reteach how to write any of the phonograms which are difficult. Break down each step and have the student repeat the short, bold directions aloud.

"Phonogram Tight Rope" on page 24
"Write and Erase" on page 29
"Optional Blind Writing" on page 40
"Phonogram Baseball" on page 54

Teacher Tip

Students who struggle with handwriting should practice writing using large motor movements. It is also beneficial for these students to recite the bold, rhythmic directions aloud when writing.

Phonograms

"Teacher Trouble" on page 10
"Phonogram Arcade Race" on page 16
"Phonogram Tight Rope" on page 24
"Classroom: Phonogram Stop and Go" on page 24
"Phonogram Reading Race" on page 44
"Phonogram Target" on page 48
"Phonogram Baseball" on page 54

High Frequency Words

Write the high frequency words from 42.3 and 48.3 on slips of paper. Ask the student to choose a word, read it, then crumple it up and try to make a basket.

Slips of paper
Basket

Objectives

PHONEMIC AWARENESS: Review syllables.

PHONOGRAM: Learn er .

HANDWRITING: Learn uppercase R .

SPELLING: her, green, sick, feet, check

Materials

NEEDED: LOE whiteboard, Basic Phonogram Flash Cards er and r , Tactile Card ℛ or R , two sets of Phonogram Game Cards, scissors, a box or basket, bag

OPTIONAL: Phonogram Game Tiles, book from book list

Phonograms

The Phonogram er

Show the Phonogram Card er .

This says /er/. What does it say? **/er/**
Write /er/ three times on your whiteboard.

The sound /er/

Show the Phonogram Card r .

What does this say? **/r/**

Show the Phonogram Card er .

What does this say? **/er/**
How are these sounds different?
You cannot sing /r/. /er/ can be sung.

Whiteboard

Basic Phonogram Flash Cards er and r

Speech Tip

Many students cannot say either /r/ or /er/. Try the following tips for helping students pronounce these sounds more clearly.

/r/ Use your hand to demonstrate how the tongue bunches up and pulls back to say /r/. Ask the child to make the shape with her hand, then to try to make her tongue into the same shape.

/er/ Have the child lie on her back while saying /r/. Let the tongue relax further back. Practice sustaining the sound by saying /ger.../ and growling.

Phonogram Practice

Go Fish

Choose 20-30 matching phonogram pairs. Deal five cards per player. Place the remaining cards in the middle of the table face down and spread them out into a "fishing pond." The first player chooses another player to ask, "Do you have a __?" Students should ask for a phonogram that matches one in their hand by saying the sound(s). If the answer is "yes," the asking player receives the card and lays down the matched pair. The asking player then repeats her turn. If the answer is "no," the player who was asked should say, "Go Fish."

The asking player then draws a card from the pond. If a match is found, it is laid down and the asking player repeats her turn. If no match is found, play moves to the next player on the left. Continue to play until all the cards have been matched. The player with the most matches wins.

2 sets of Phonogram Game Cards

Challenge

Include three or four matches of each phonogram card in the pile. Students must then find sets of three or four in order to lay them down.

Handwriting

Writing Uppercase R

51.1 Uppercase R – page 55

Compare and contrast the upper- and lowercase /r/ in a bookface font and in the handwriting font.

Let's learn how to write the uppercase /r/.

Demonstrate how to write uppercase /r/ using 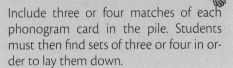 ℛ or ℛ .

Whiteboard
Tactile Card ℛ or ℛ

Start halfway between the midline and the top line. ①**Curve** up to the top line, ②**straight** to the baseline, ③slide **up** to the top line, ④**circle** around to the midline, ⑤touch, ⑥**kick** down to the baseline.

Start at the top line. ①**Straight** to the baseline, ②slide **up** to the top line, ③**circle** around to the midline, ④touch, ⑤**kick** down to the baseline.

Write the uppercase /r/ three times on the Tactile Card or in the air, using your pointer finger.

Write the uppercase /r/ three times on your whiteboard.
Which one sits on the baseline the best?
Which one looks most like the Tactile Card?
Put a smiley face next to the best /r/.

Writing on Paper

Book List

Bob Books Set 1
Peg and Ted

51.1 Uppercase R – page 55

Write uppercase /r/ three times on your favorite line size.

51.2 Match the Sound – page 56

I will read a phonogram. Circle all the ways that phonogram is written.

1.   /n/
2.   /s-z/
3.   /t/
4.   /m/
5.   /ă-ā-ä/
6.   /r/

Phonemic Awareness

Syllables

What is a syllable? *It is the beat in words.*
How did you learn to count the syllables? *Put my hand under my chin and feel how many times my mouth opens to say the vowel sound.*

Multi-Sensory Fun

March or stomp your feet to the syllables as you hum them.

Today we will learn a new way to count syllables. I will say a word; you need to hum it. For example, if I say, *tiger*, then hum *tiger*: /hm-hm/. How many times do you say /hm/ when humming *tiger*? *two*

Tiger has two syllables.

rocket   */hm-hm/ two syllables*
carpenter   */hm-hm-hm/ three syllables*
telephone   */hm-hm-hm/ three syllables*
dinner   */hm-hm/ two syllables*

panther   */hm-hm/ two syllables*
afternoon   */hm-hm-hm/ three syllables*
coin   */hm/ one syllable*
marble   */hm-hm/ two syllables*

Spelling

Spelling List

Teach the words using the steps for Spelling Analysis. Direct students to write the words on their whiteboards or with Phonogram Game Tiles.

	Word	Sentence	Say to Spell	Markings	Spelling Hints
1.	her	*Her house is around the corner.*	her	h<u>er</u>	Underline /er/.
2.	green	*The green coat is warmer.*	grēn	gr<u>ee</u>n	Underline E double E, which always says /ē/.
3.	sick	*She feels sick.*	sĭk	si<u>ck</u>	Underline two-letter /k/, used only after a single, short vowel.
4.	feet	*The duck has webbed feet.*	fēt	f<u>ee</u>t	Underline E double E, which always says /ē/.
5.	check	*Please check on your brother.*	chĕk	<u>ch</u>e<u>ck</u>	Underline /ch/. Underline /k/. CK, two-letter /k/ is used only after a single, short vowel.

Reading

High Frequency Words

51.3 Reading Basketball – pages 57-58

Cut out the words. Fold each one in half and put them in a bag. Direct the student to draw a word, read it, and then crumple it up and shoot a basket. Give the student one point if the word is read correctly, and one point if she makes a basket.

Scissors

Box or basket

Bag

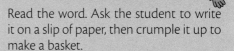

Challenge

Read the word. Ask the student to write it on a slip of paper, then crumple it up to make a basket.

Teacher Tip

If you are laminating your High Frequency Word Cards for ongoing use, write the words on slips of paper for this activity.

Objectives

PHONEMIC AWARENESS: Review syllables. Practice letter names.

PHONOGRAM: Learn wh .

HANDWRITING: Learn uppercase W .

SPELLING: when, which, get, stand, queen

Materials

NEEDED: LOE whiteboard, Basic Phonogram Flash Card wh and all the phonograms learned so far, Tactile Card *W* or *W* , timer, magnetic upper- and lowercase letters for A, B, D, F, H, M, N, P, R, S, T, cloth bag

OPTIONAL: Phonogram Game Tiles

Phonograms

The Phonogram wh

Show the Phonogram Card wh .

> This says /wh/. What does it say? */wh/*
> Write /wh/ three times on your whiteboard.

Whiteboard
Basic Phonogram Flash Card wh

Speech Tip

Many English dialects do not distinguish WH from W. However, in some regions the airy /h/ is clearly heard. If you hear W and WH as distinct, teach them as distinct sounds. If you hear them as the same sound, /w/, teach them as two spellings for the sound /w/.

Handwriting

Writing Uppercase W

Whiteboard
Tactile Card 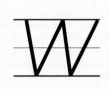 or W

52.1 Uppercase W – page 59

Compare and contrast the upper- and lowercase /w/ in a bookface font and in the handwriting font.

Let's learn how to write the uppercase /w/.

Demonstrate how to write uppercase /w/ using W or W .

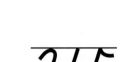

Start halfway between the midline and the top line. ①**Curve** up to the top line, ②**down** to the baseline, ③**swing** up to the top line, ④**down** to the baseline, ⑤**swing** up to the top line, ⑥**dip** below the top line.

Start at the top line. ①**Kick** down to the baseline, ②**angle up** to the top line ③**kick** down to the baseline, ④**angle up** to the top line.

Write uppercase /w/ three times on the Tactile Card or in the air, using your pointer finger.

Write uppercase /w/ three times on your whiteboard.
Which one sits on the baseline the best?
Which one looks most like the Tactile Card?
Put a smiley face next to the best /w/.

Writing on Paper

52.1 Uppercase W – page 59

Write uppercase /w/ three times on your favorite line size.

Phonogram Practice

Timed Phonogram Reading

How fast do you think you can read all the phonograms we have learned? *answers will vary*

I will set a timer and see if you are right. Ready, set, go!

All the Basic Phonogram Flash Cards learned so far

Timer

Letter Matching Game

Put the letters in a cloth bag. Direct the student:

Draw a letter out of the bag. Then say the letter's name and the sound(s). Place the letter on the table and draw the next one. If you find one that matches a letter you already have on the table, put them next to one another.

Magnetic upper- and lowercase letters for A, B, D, F, H, M, N, P, R, S, T

Cloth bag

Phonemic Awareness

Syllables

What is a syllable? *It is the rhythm of words.*

What are two ways we can count how many syllables are in a word? *Put my hand under my chin and feel how many times my mouth opens to say the vowel sound. Hum the word.*

How many syllables are there in *eagle*? */hm-hm/ two syllables*

52.2 Syllables – page 60

Look at the pictures on the page. Say the name of the animal. Then hum the animal name. Circle the number of syllables in the word.

Spelling

Spelling List

Teach the words for students to write on their whiteboards. Use the steps for Spelling Analysis.

	Word	Sentence	Say to Spell	Markings	Spelling Hints
1.	when	*When will we leave?*	whĕn	<u>wh</u>en	Underline /wh/.
2.	which	*Which hat is yours?*	whĭch	<u>wh</u>i<u>ch</u>	Underline /wh/. Underline /ch/.
3.	get	*Did you get one?*	gĕt	get	All first sounds.
4.	stand	*We need to stand in line.*	stănd	stand	All first sounds.
5.	queen	*Long live the queen.*	kwēn	<u>queen</u>	Underline /kw/. Underline E double E, which always says /ē/.

Reading

Questions

Write the following sentences on the board. "Did he run fast?" "He did run fast."

Read the first sentence. *Did he run fast?*

Read the second sentence. *He did run fast.*

What is different about these two sentences? *One is asking a question. The other gives the answer. The order of the words is different.*

Point to the period and then the question mark.

This is called a period. We use it at the end of a sentence when we are telling someone information.

This is called a question mark. When do we use a question mark? *When we are asking a question.*

I will read both the sentence and the question aloud to you. Listen to my voice. What does my voice do when I am asking a question? *Your voice goes higher at the end.*

Now listen to me read the question without letting my voice go up in pitch at the end.

Read the question as if it is a statement.

Does that sound right? *no*

I will write another question on the board. Read it aloud. *Did he brush the cat?*

52.3 Matching Questions – pages 61-62

Read each question aloud. Look at the picture. Read the answer. Circle the correct picture.

Objectives

PHONEMIC AWARENESS: To make a word plural, just add -S.

PHONOGRAM: Learn oy and oi .

SPELLING RULE: English words do not end in I, U, V, or J.

HANDWRITING: Learn uppercase U .

SPELLING: boy, coin, feed, joy, bunch

Materials

NEEDED: LOE whiteboard, Basic Phonogram Flash Cards previously learned and oi and oy , Tactile Card $\mathcal{U}$ or U , timer, blocks

OPTIONAL: Phonogram Game Tiles, objects in the room that represent words, playdough, popsicle stick

Spelling Rule

English Words Do Not End in I, U, V, or J

Today we will learn a new rule about words. I will say it one time, then I want you to say it with me. English words do not end in I, U, V, or J.

Write I, U, V, and J on the board.

Let's shout the rule. *English words do not end in I, U, V, or J!*
Let's say it in a mean voice. *English words do not end in I, U, V, or J.*
Let's say it in a sweet voice. *English words do not end in I, U, V, or J.*

Phonograms

The Phonograms oi and oy

Show the Phonogram Card oi .
　　This says /oi/. What does it say? */oi/*

Show the Phonogram Card oy .
　　This says /oi/. What does it say? */oi/*

Show the Phonogram Cards oi and oy .
　　What is the same about these two phonograms? *They both say /oi/. They both start with an O.*
　　What is different about them? *One ends with an I and one ends with a Y.*
　　Which one may I use at the end of the word? *oy*
　　Why? *English words do not end in I, U, V or J.*

　　Which one will I use to spell *boy*? *oy*
　　Why? *English words do not end in I.*
　　What about in *toy*? *oy*
　　Why? *English words do not end in I.*

　　Write /oi/ that you may NOT use at the end of English words on your whiteboard.
　　Write /oi/ that you MAY use at the end of English words on your whiteboard.

Direct the students to write one or the other quickly on their board and show it to you.

Whiteboard
Basic Phonogram Flash Cards oi and oy

Teacher Tip

From now on we will refer to OY as /oi/ that you may use at the end of English words and OI as /oi/ that you may not use at the end of English words.

Phonogram Practice

Phonogram Challenge

Choose a time between 1-3 minutes. Explain that you will set a timer, then select a phonogram and read it without showing the phonogram to the student. The student needs to write the phonogram on his whiteboard. If he gets it right, you will put the phonogram card in one pile. If he gets it wrong, you will place it in a different pile. Count how many points he has after the timer goes off.

Whiteboard
Timer
Basic Phonogram Flash Cards

Classroom: Phonogram Teams

Divide the students into pairs. Provide a stack of phonogram cards to practice. One student selects a card, reads the sound(s), the other student writes the phonogram on his whiteboard. If he writes it correctly, the team gets one point. If not, the card goes to the bottom of the pile.

Whiteboard for each team

Timer

Basic Phonogram Flash Cards learned
    so far

Phonemic Awareness

Plurals

Place a block on the table and say out loud:
    block

Put a second block on the table.
    blocks

Take one block off the table.
    block

Put the second block back on the table.

    blocks

    How does the word *block* change when I have more than one? *We add a /s/ sound to the end.*

    When we have more than one of something it is called a plural. Say plural with me. *plural*

    What does plural mean? *more than one*

    Help me to sound out *block* as I write it on the board

    /b-l-ŏ-k/

Write *block* on the board.

    Now let's write *blocks*. /b-l-ŏ-k-s/

Write *blocks* on the board.

    What did I add to the end of *block* to make it plural? *a /s-z/*

Point to your leg.

    This is my leg.

    I have two legs.

    What sound does /s-z/ make at the end of *legs*? /z/

    Sound out *legs* as I write it on the board. /l-ĕ-g-z/

Write *legs* on the board.

    Sometimes the S says /s/ and sometimes it says /z/.

    This leads us to the new spelling rule: To make a noun plural, just add the ending -S!

    Let's shout the rule! *To make a noun plural, just add the ending -S!*

Blocks

Objects in the room

Multi-Sensory Fun

Ask the students to go on a plural hunt. Find objects around the room that are plural. Say the plural aloud emphasizing the /s/ or /z/ sound at the end.

Teacher Tip

If a student asks about a plural where ES gets added, share the whole rule: *To make a noun plural add the ending -S, unless the word hisses or changes; then add -ES. Some nouns have no change or an irregular spelling.* Then simply explain how the word relates to the full rule.

Challenge

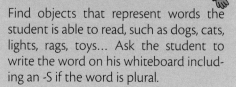

Find objects that represent words the student is able to read, such as dogs, cats, lights, rags, toys... Ask the student to write the word on his whiteboard including an -S if the word is plural.

Let's whisper the rule. *To make a noun plural, just add the ending -S.*

53.1 Plurals – page 63

Look at the pictures on your worksheet. Point to each picture that shows a plural. *cats, trees, toys*
What does plural mean? *more than one*
What do we need to add to the end of the word to show that it is plural? */s-z/*
Add a /s-z/ to each of the plural words.

Handwriting

Writing Uppercase U

53.2 Uppercase U – page 64

Compare and contrast the upper- and lowercase /ŭ-ū-ö-ü/ in
a bookface font and in the handwriting font.

Let's learn how to write the uppercase /ŭ-ū-ö-ü/.
Demonstrate how to write uppercase /ŭ-ū-ö-ü/ using .

Whiteboard
Tactile Card

Start halfway between the mid-line and the top line. ①**Curve** up to the top line, ②**down** to the baseline, ③**swing** up to the top line, ④**down** to the baseline.

Start at the top line. ①**Down** to the baseline, ②**swing tall** to the top line, ③**straight** to the baseline.

Write uppercase /ŭ-ū-ö-ü/ three times on the Tactile Card or in the air, using your pointer finger.

Write uppercase /ŭ-ū-ö-ü/ three times on your whiteboard.
Which one looks most like the Tactile Card?
Put a smiley face next to the best /ŭ-ū-ö-ü/.

Writing on Paper

53.2 Uppercase U – page 64

Write uppercase /ŭ-ū-ö-ü/ three times on your favorite line size.

Multi-Sensory Fun

Provide students with playdough and a popsicle stick. Have the students roll out the playdough and write the uppercase phonograms in the dough.

Spelling

Spelling List

Teach the words using the steps for Spelling Analysis. Direct students to write the words on their whiteboards or with Phonogram Game Tiles.

Word	Sentence	Say to Spell	Markings	Spelling Hints
1. boy	*The boy threw the ball.*	boi	b<u>oy</u>	Underline the /oi/ that we may use at the end of English words. English words do not end in I.
2. coin	*I found a coin on the sidewalk.*	koin	c<u>oi</u>n	Underline the /oi/ that we may not use at the end of English words.
3. feed	*Let's feed the ducks.*	fēd	f<u>ee</u>d	Underline E double E, which always says /ē/.
4. joy	*It has been a joy to have you in my class.*	joi	j<u>oy</u>	Underline the /oi/ that we may use at the end of English words. English words do not end in I
5. bunch	*She picked a bunch of flowers.*	bŭnch	bun<u>ch</u>	Underline /ch/.

boy

The first word is *boy*. The boy threw the ball. *boy*
Place your hand under your chin and say, "boy." How many syllables in *boy*? **boy, one**
Let's sound it out.
/b-oi/
What kind of /oi/ will we use? **oy**
Why? *Because English words do not end in I, U, V, or J.*
Now write *boy*.
The student writes *boy* on his whiteboard.

It is now my turn to write *boy*. Sound it out as I write it.
The teacher writes *boy* on the board.
What does this say? */b-oi/ boy*
Let's underline the /oi/ to help us remember that the O and Y work together to say /oi/.

coin

The second word is *coin*. I found a coin on the sidewalk. *coin*
Place your hand under your chin and say, "coin." How many
syllables in *coin*? **coin, one**

Let's sound it out.

Segment the word along with the students, speaking the
sounds softly to support them as they sound it out and adding the cue for how they will spell /k/:

/k (use /k-s/) *-oi-n/*

What kind of /oi/ will we use? **oi**

Why? **Because the /oi/ is not at the end of the word.**

Now write *coin*.

The student writes *coin* on his whiteboard.

It is now my turn to write *coin*. Sound it out as I write it. **/k-oi-n/**

The teacher writes *coin* on the board.

What does this say? **/k-oi-n/ coin**

Let's underline the /oi/ to help us remember that the O and I work together to say /oi/.

Teacher Tip

Remind students to use /k-s/ as they spell coin.

Reading

Find It!

53.3 Find It! – page 65

Read the word. Look at the picture. Find the object in the picture. Notice that some of the words end with
a /s-z/. This means they are plural. When the word is plural, there will be more than one in the picture.
Count how many you find and write the number in the blank.

LESSON 54

Objectives

PHONEMIC AWARENESS: Review long and short vowel sounds.

PHONOGRAM: Learn ai and ay .

SPELLING RULE: English words do not end in I, U, V, or J.

HANDWRITING: Learn uppercase I .

SPELLING: play, tail, day, sleep, cheer

Materials

NEEDED: LOE whiteboard, Basic Phonogram Flash Cards ay and ai , Tactile Card *I* or I , two sets of Phonogram Game Cards

OPTIONAL: Sensory box with sand, rice, or cornmeal; Phonogram Game Tiles; highlighter; a book from the book list

Phonemic Awareness

Long and Short Vowels

Whiteboard

54.1 Long and Short Vowels – page 66

I will say a vowel sound. Write it on your whiteboard, including the mark that tells whether it is long or short. I will do one example on the board.

/ŏ/

Write ŏ on the board.

Each time you get a short sound right, you may cross out a short box on the chart. Each time you get a long sound right you may cross out a long box. When all the boxes are crossed off, you will be finished with your practice.

/ă/	/ā/
/ĕ/	/ī/
/ē/	/ū/...
/ī/	

Spelling Rule

English Words Do Not End in I, U, V, or J

Let's practice our new spelling rule, English words do not end in I, U, V, or J.

Write I, U, V, and J on the board.

Let's whisper the rule. *English words do not end in I, U, V, or J.*
Let's sing it. *English words do not end in I, U, V, or J.*
Let's say it in a grumpy voice. *English words do not end in I, U, V, or J.*

Phonograms

The Phonograms ai and ay

Show the Phonogram Card ai .
This says /ā/. What does it say? */ā/*

Show the Phonogram Card ay .
This says /ā/. What does it say? */ā/*

Show the Phonogram Cards ai and ay .

What is the same about these two phonograms? *They both say /ā/. They both start with an A.*
What is different about them? *One ends in I and one ends in Y.*
Which one may I use at the end of the word? *ay*
Why? *English words do not end in I, U, V or J.*
Which one will I use to spell *may*? *ay*
Why? *English words do not end in I.*
Which one will I use to spell *say*? *ay*
Why? *English words do not end in I.*

Write two-letter /ā/ that you may NOT use at the end of English words on your whiteboard.
Write two-letter /ā/ that you MAY use at the end of English words on your whiteboard.

Direct the students to write one or the other quickly on their board and show it to you.

Whiteboard
Basic Phonogram Flash Cards ai and
ay

Phonogram Practice

Last One!

Choose matching sets of 10-15 phonograms which need additional practice. Shuffle the chosen phonograms and game cards. Deal seven cards to each player. Place the remaining cards in a draw pile. Turn one card face up to form the discard pile.

2 sets of Phonogram Game Cards

2 Wild cards

2 Draw Two cards

2 Reverse cards

Take turns discarding a card that matches the card on the discard pile either in color or in phonogram. The student must read the phonogram's sound(s) as he discards. If the player misreads the sound(s), he must keep his card, and play moves to the next player. If a player does not have a matching card, he must draw one card from the draw pile. Play then continues with the next player.

Players may play a *Draw Two* or *Reverse* card only if it matches in color. If a *Draw Two* card is played, the next person must draw 2 cards from the draw pile. He may not lay down a card. If a *Reverse* card is played, the play switches directions. If a *Wild* card is played, the player may select a new color. A player wins when he has discarded all his cards.

Variation 1: For simpler play, remove the *Reverse* and/or *Draw Two* cards.

Handwriting

Writing Uppercase I

54.2 Uppercase I – page 67

Compare and contrast the upper- and lowercase /ĭ-ī-ē-y/ in a bookface font and in the handwriting font.

Whiteboard

Tactile Card or I

Let's learn how to write the uppercase /ĭ-ī-ē-y/.
Demonstrate how to write uppercase /ĭ-ī-ē-y/ using or I .

Start halfway between the baseline and the midline. ①**Out**, ②**roll** down to the baseline, ③**loop** up to the top line, ④**down** to the baseline.

Start at the top line. ①**Straight** to the baseline, ②pick up the pencil, ③**cross** at the top line, ④pick up the pencil, ⑤**cross** at the baseline.

Write uppercase /ĭ-ī-ē-y/ three times on the Tactile Card or in the air, using your pointer finger.

Write uppercase /ĭ-ī-ē-y/ three times on your whiteboard.
Which one looks most like the Tactile Card?
Put a smiley face next to the best /ĭ-ī-ē-y/.

Writing on Paper

54.2 Uppercase I – page 67

Write uppercase /ĭ-ī-ē-y/ three times on your favorite line size.

Multi-Sensory Fun

Practice writing the uppercase phonograms in a sensory box filled with sand, rice, or cornmeal.

Spelling

Spelling List

Teach the words using the steps for Spelling Analysis. Direct students to write the words on their whiteboards or with Phonogram Game Tiles.

Word	Sentence	Say to Spell	Markings	Spelling Hints
1. play	*Do you want to play a game?*	plā	pl<u>ay</u>	Underline /ā/ that may be used at the end of the word. English words do not end in I, U, V, or J.
2. tail	*The dog wagged his tail.*	tāl	t<u>ai</u>l	Underline /ā/ that may not be used at the end of the word.
3. day	*Which day are you going to the movie?*	dā	d<u>ay</u>	Underline /ā/ that may be used at the end of the word. English words do not end in I, U, V, or J.
4. sleep	*Sleep well.*	slēp	sl<u>ee</u>p	Underline E double E, which always says /ē/.
5. cheer	*They cheer for the star player.*	chēr	<u>ch</u><u>ee</u>r	Underline /ch/. Underline E double E, which always says /ē/.

Reading

Matching

54.3 Matching – pages 68-69

Read the sentence. Draw a line to match it to the correct picture.

Multi-Sensory Fun

Direct the student to look through the words and underline or highlight each multi-letter phonogram.

Book List

Bob Books Set 1
    Dot and the Dog

Objectives

PHONEMIC AWARENESS: Compare /f/ and /v/.

HANDWRITING: Learn to write ⬚J⬚.

SPELLING: of, as, has, free, click

READER 3

Materials

NEEDED: LOE whiteboard, Tactile Card ⬚ or ⬚ , two sets of Phonogram Game Cards, game board pieces, a red and a green die, Phonogram Chart, Basic Phonogram Flash Cards ⬚f⬚ and ⬚v⬚ , Lazy Vowel Chart, Reader 3

OPTIONAL: Sidewalk chalk, Phonogram Game Tiles, a book from the book list

Handwriting

Writing Uppercase ⬚J⬚

55.1 Uppercase J – page 70

Compare and contrast the upper- and lowercase /j/ in a bookface font and in the handwriting font.

Let's learn how to write the uppercase /j/.
Demonstrate how to write uppercase /j/ using ⬚ or ⬚ .

Whiteboard
Tactile Card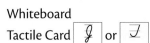

 *Start at the baseline.* [1]Tight **circle** around to the top line, [2]**drop** down halfway below the baseline, [3]**swoop**.

 Start at the top line. [1]**Drop** to the baseline, [2]**swoop**.

Write uppercase /j/ three times on the Tactile Card or in the air, using your pointer finger.

Write uppercase /j/ three times on your whiteboard.
Which one looks most like the Tactile Card?
Put a smiley face next to the best /j/.

Writing on Paper

55.1 Uppercase – page 70

Write uppercase /j/ three times on your favorite line size.

55.2 Matching – page 71

Match the uppercase and lowercase letters.

Phonogram Practice

Phonogram Boat Race

55.3 Phonogram Boat Race – page 72

Mix two sets of game cards together. Place the cards in a pile face down. Place one game piece per player at Go.

Ask the child to roll both dice. Note the number on the green die. Select that number of cards off the top of the stack and read the sound(s). If the student reads them correctly, he may move his piece the same number of spaces forward. If he misreads a sound, he should move his piece backwards the number of spaces shown on the red die. The first player to reach Stop wins.

For additional challenge, add in the *Go Back One Space* and *Go Back Two Spaces* cards.

2 sets of Phonogram Game Cards
1 red die
1 green die
Game pieces
Go Back One card
Go Back Two card

Teacher Tip

Save the Phonogram Boat Race game board for use in Lesson 56.

Phonemic Awareness

ABC Song

Let's sing the ABC song as we point to each of the phonograms.

Phonogram Chart

/f/ and /v/

Show the Phonogram Card f .

Basic Phonogram Flash Cards f and v

What does this say? */f/*

How do you say the sound /f/? What is your mouth doing? *My top teeth are touching my lip and I blow air out.*

Place your hand on your throat as you say /f/. Is it a voiced or an unvoiced sound? *unvoiced*

Show the Phonogram Card v .

What does this say? */v/*

How do you say the sound /v/? What is your mouth doing? *My top teeth are touching my lip and I blow air out.*

Place your hand on your throat as you say /v/. Is it a voiced or an unvoiced sound? *voiced*

Show the Phonogram Cards f and v .

How are these sounds the same? *My mouth is in the same place to make both /f/ and /v/.*

How are they different? *For /v/ I turn my voicebox on. /f/ is unvoiced.*

One of our words in this lesson will use this information. Raise your hand when you think you know why we compared /f/ and /v/ today.

Speech Tip

For more information about how to make speech sounds, see *Eliciting Sounds: Techniques and Strategies for Clinicians 2nd Edition*, by Wayne A. Secord, Cengage Learning 2007.

Spelling

Spelling List

Teach the words using the steps for Spelling Analysis. Direct students to write the words on their whiteboards or with Phonogram Game Tiles.

Word	Sentence	Say to Spell	Markings	Spelling Hints
1. of	*I cannot think of the answer.*	ŏv	^xof	The /ŏ/ is saying the lazy schwa sound. Put an X over /v/. This word is a true exception. This is the only word where F says /v/. Discuss how /f/ and /v/ are a voiced and unvoiced pair.
2. as	*I have as many points as he has.*	ăz	as²	Put a 2 over the /z/. /s-z/ said its second sound /z/.
3. has	*She has a big dog.*	hăz	has²	Put a 2 over the /z/. /s-z/ said its second sound /z/.
4. free	*Everything in this box is free.*	frē	fr<u>ee</u>	Underline /ē/. E double E always says /ē/.
5. click	*Click on the picture to hear the sound.*	klĭk	cli<u>ck</u>	Underline two-letter /k/. Used only after a single, short vowel.

of

The first word is *of*. I cannot think of the answer. *of*
Let's say *of* together. **of**
How many sounds are in the word *of*? **/ə-v/ two**
Both sounds in this word have a problem. It is a two sound word, with two problems.
The first problem is that we have a lazy vowel sound.
A few lessons ago, we talked about a lazy vowel sound. What is the sound that vowels say when they are lazy? *schwa /ə/*
Let's read the list of lazy vowel words we have collected: **the, a**
I will add one more word to our list. Then we will talk about it.

Write *of* on the Lazy Vowel Chart.

Listen to the word again. Listen for the lazy vowel sound. *of*
Which sound is the lazy vowel? **The first one. /ŭ/**
Now let's look at *of*.

Lazy Vowel Chart

Teacher Tip

Schwa is an unstressed vowel sound. The schwa usually sounds like a short /ŭ/. For example, the A in <u>a</u>bout.

Point to the O.

What would this first phonogram say if we pronounced it clearly? **/ŏ/**

To help us remember which vowel is saying the lazy sound, we will say to spell /ŏv/.

We said the word has two problems. Listen as I say the word and see if you can find the second problem. *of* **The F is saying /v/, not /f/.**

This is the only word in all of English where F says /v/! Do you think that when someone wrote this word it is possible that people may have said, "/o-f/" not "/o-v/?"

Why do you think it may have changed from /f/ to /v/? **/v/ is voiced, /f/ is not voiced.**

This is one of the strangest English words we will ever learn. I want you to write *of* on your whiteboard three times. After you write it, read it.

Reading

Reader

Take out Reader 3. Ask the student to read the title and each page aloud.

When the student has finished the book, ask:

What are the toys waiting for? *The toys are waiting for the boy to go to sleep.*

Why? *They want to play.*

In real life, can toys play on their own? *no*

The toys are acting like people. When objects or animals act like people in stories, it is called *personification*. That is a big word. I will say it again. Can you hear the word *person* in the middle? Personification.

What do you think personification means?

Personification means that toys, animals, or other objects are acting like persons or like people.

Can you think of other stories or movies where toys are personified?

Can you think of other stories or movies where an animal is personified?

Reader 3

Book List

Bob Books Set 1
Jig and Mag
10 Cut-Ups

REVIEW C

Area	Skill	Mastery
Phonemic Awareness	Count syllables.	2
	Make words plural by adding an -S.	1
Handwriting	Write uppercase N, A, D, B, P.	2
	Write uppercase R, W, U, I, J.	2
Phonograms	Read ck, igh, ch, ee.	1
	Read er, wh, oi, oy, ai, ay.	2
Reading	Read short sentences.	2
	Read the high frequency words.	1

Skills with a 1 should be mastered before students move on to the next lesson. For skills marked with a 2, students should demonstrate familiarity but not necessarily answer all the questions correctly. These skills will be practiced extensively in the upcoming lessons.

Phonemic Awareness Assessment

Syllables

C.1 Syllables – page 73

Look at the picture. Say the word. Count the syllables. Circle the correct number.

Plurals

C.2 Plurals – page 74

Look at the picture. Add an -S if it is needed to make the word plural.

Handwriting Assessment

Handwriting

C.3 Handwriting – page 75

Write one of each phonogram on your favorite line size.

Multi-Sensory Fun

If the student is not ready to write on paper, show the student the phonogram card and have him write the phonogram on a whiteboard or in a sensory box.

Phonogram Assessment

Phonogram Assessment

Ask the student to read each of the following phonogram cards: ck, igh, ch, ee, er, wh, oi, oy, ai, ay

Basic Phonogram Flash Cards

ck	igh	ch	ee	er
wh	oi	oy	ai	ay

What's That Phonogram?

Highlighter

C.4 What's That Phonogram? – pages 76-77

On your page are groups of four phonograms. I will say a phonogram's sound(s). Color the phonogram with your highlighter.

1. /k/ two-letter /k/
2. /er/ the /er/ of her
3. /ā/ two-letter /ā/ that you may use at the end of English words.
4. /ī/ three-letter /ī/
5. /ch-k-sh/
6. /ē/ double /ē/ always says /ē/
7. /wh/
8. /oi/ that you may NOT use at the end of English words.
9. /ā/ two-letter /ā/ that you may NOT use at the end of English words.
10. /oy/ that you may use at the end of English words.

Reading Assessment

Reading

C.5 Reading – pages 78-79

Read the sentence. Match it to the correct picture.

High Frequency Words

C.6 High Frequency Words – page 80

Read each word.

Teacher Tip

Ask the student to read the sentences aloud. Which phonograms and words did he struggle with?

Multi-Sensory Fun

Write the words on index cards. Line them up against the wall. Ask children to choose a word, read it, then zoom a matchbox car at it.

Practice Ideas

Syllables

"Counting Syllables" on page 12 of the Teacher's Manual
"Syllables" on page 15
"Syllables" on page 23
"Syllables" on page 68

Handwriting

Using the Tactile Cards, reteach how to write any of the phonograms which are difficult. Break down each step and have the student repeat the short, bold directions aloud.

"Optional Blind Writing" on page 40
"Phonogram Baseball" on page 54
"Phonogram Challenge" on page 75

Teacher Tip

Students who struggle with handwriting should practice writing using large motor movements. It is also beneficial for these students to recite the bold, rhythmic directions aloud when writing.

Phonograms

"Phonogram Reading Race" on page 44
"Phonogram Target" on page 48
"Phonogram Baseball" on page 54
"Go Fish" on page 67
"Timed Phonogram Reading" on page 72
"Last One!" on page 82
"Phonogram Boat Race" on page 86

High Frequency Words

Play Phonogram Boat Race. Place all the high frequency words upside down in a pile. Place the game pieces at Go. Roll the die. Choose the number of word cards from the pile. If the student reads them all correctly, move forward the number of spaces shown on the die.

High Frequency Word Cards from 42.3, 48.3, and 51.3
Phonogram Boat Race board from 55.3
Game pieces
Die

High frequency words from 42.3, 48.3, and 51.3:
and, ask, best, drink, fast, help, jump, just, must, stop, that, them, think, this, wish, with, fish, hand,
a, be, go, he, his, is, stick, light, me, night, right, no, she, so, the, we, black, back, green, has, her,
keep, much, pick, see, sleep, then, three, went, duck, feet, milk, nest, seed, sheep, tree

LESSON 56

Objectives

PHONEMIC AWARENESS: Practice long and short vowel sounds.

SPELLING RULE: The vowel says its long sound because of the E.

SPELLING: made, name, stop, time, may

Materials

NEEDED: LOE whiteboard, two sets of Phonogram Game Cards, game board from worksheet 55.3, game board pieces, a red and a green die, Basic Phonogram Flash Cards `a`, `e`, `i`, `o`, `u`, Phonogram Game Tiles, table, blankets, bag

Phonogram Practice

Phonogram Boat Race

55.3 Phonogram Boat Race – page 72

Mix two sets of game cards together. Place the cards in a pile face down. Place one game piece per player at Go.

Ask the child to roll both dice. Note the number on the green die. Select that number of cards off the top of the stack and read the sound(s). If the student reads them correctly, he may move his piece the same number of spaces forward. If he misreads a sound, he should move his piece backwards the number of spaces shown on the red die. The first player to reach Stop wins.

Game board from worksheet 55.3

2 sets of Phonogram Game Cards that
   have been learned so far

1 red die

1 green die

Game pieces

Go Back One card

Go Back Two card

Multi-Sensory Fun

Ask the student to write the phonogram on a whiteboard as he reads each one.

Challenge

Add in the *Go Back One Space* and *Go Back Two Spaces* cards.

Phonemic Awareness

Long and Short Vowels

Show the students the vowel phonograms. Ask the students to read the short sounds. Then ask them to read the long sounds.

Basic Phonogram Flash Cards a ,
e , i , o , u

> Today we will play a game. I want you to stand up. If you hear a long sound, I want you to stretch your arms out wide like the straight line we put over the long sounds.

> If you hear a short sound, I want you to kneel and form your arms into a curve over your head, like the breve we write over the short sounds.

Say short and long sounds as the students practice.

Multi-Sensory Fun

If a student struggles to hear the difference between a long and short sound, have him say each sound, then describe the difference in how his mouth forms the sound. Play the game again, this time having the student repeat the target sound aloud before deciding if it is long or short.

Spelling Rule

Silent Final E

> Today we will learn a new rule for when a vowel will say its long sound. You will be a spelling detective. I will write a word using phonogram tiles. I want you to read the word. Then I will change the word and read it to you. Raise your hand when you have discovered what is changing and why.

Phonogram Game Tiles

| c | a | p | *cap*

Add an | e | and read *cape.*

| c | a | p | e |

Continue until the child identifies: *the vowel says its long sound because of the E.*

| b | i | t | | b | i | t | e |

| n | o | t | | n | o | t | e |

> Does the E make a sound? *no*
> We call this a silent E because it is a letter that is silent.

Hold your finger up to your lips to signal quiet or silent.

> But does the silent E have a job? *yes*
> What is its job? *It makes the vowel say its long sound.*
> Whenever we have a silent E we always need to ask, "What is its job?" As we continue we will learn eight

more silent E jobs. Today we have learned one job: "The vowel says its long sound because of the E."

Let's shout the rule: *The vowel says its long sound because of the E.*

Let's whisper the rule: *The vowel says its long sound because of the E.*

Ask the student to read the following words as you form them.

r	a	t

r	a	t	e

t	a	p

t	a	p	e

r	o	b

r	o	b	e

r	i	d

r	i	d	e

m	a	d

m	a	d	e

Spelling

Spelling List

Teach the words using the steps for Spelling Analysis. Direct students to write the words on their whiteboards or with Phonogram Game Tiles.

	Word	Sentence	Say to Spell	Markings	Spelling Hints
1.	made	*I made my bed today.*	mād	mad̲e̲	Put a line over the /ā/. Double underline the silent E. The vowel said its long sound because of the E.
2.	name	*What is your name?*	nām	nām̲e̲	Put a line over the /ā/. Double underline the silent E. The vowel said its long sound because of the E.
3.	stop	*Stop and look both ways.*	stŏp	stop	All first sounds.
4.	time	*What time is it?*	tīm	tīm̲e̲	Put a line over the /ī/. Double underline the silent E. The vowel said its long sound because of the E.
5.	may	*May I go outside?*	mā	may̲	Underline /ā/ that may be used at the end of the word. English words do not end in I, U, V, or J.

made

The first word is *made*. I made my bed today. *made*

Place your hand under your chin and say, "made." How many syllables in *made*? **made, one**

Let's sound it out. */m-ā-d/*

Teacher whispers: "Silent final E."

Now write *made*. Sound it out as you write it. */m-ā-d/*

The student writes *made* on his whiteboard.

It is now my turn to write *made*. Sound it out as I write it. */m-ā-d/*

The teacher writes *mad* on the board. Leave off the Silent E.

What does this say? **m-ă-d mad**

How do we change it to say *made*? **add a silent E**

Write the silent E on the board.

Let's read it together. */m-ā-d/*

When we have a silent E we will underline it twice to tell us it is silent. Why do we have a silent final E in *made*? **to make the A say its long sound /ā/**

Since A said its long sound, draw a line over it.

name

The second word is *name*. What is your name? *name*

Place your hand under your chin and say, "name." How many syllables in *name*? **name, one**

Let's sound it out. */n-ā-m/*

Teacher whispers: "Silent final E."

Now write *name*. Sound it out as you write it. */n-ā-m/*

The student writes *name* on his whiteboard.

It is now my turn to write *name*. Sound it out as I write it. */n-ā-m/*

The teacher writes *name* on the board.

What does this say? */n-ā-m/ name*

With your hand, cover up the Silent E.

Now what does it say? **năm**

Uncover the Silent E.

How will we mark a silent E? **underline it twice**

Why do we have a silent final E in *name*? **to make the A say its long sound /ā/**

Since A said its long sound, draw a line over it.

Silent E Machine

56.1 Silent E Machine – page 81

Table

Blankets

Bag

Create a "machine" by spreading blankets over a table. Cut out the word strips along the green dotted lines. Do **not** cut the solid red line. Crease the strips along the solid red line. Place them unfolded in a bag on one side of the "machine" created out of blankets and a table.

Explain to the students that today they will put words through a silent E machine. Direct the student to choose a word and read it. The child should then crawl into the "machine" and fold the word. When he emerges on the other side of the "machine" he then reads the new word with the E added.

Classroom Silent E Machine

56.1 Silent E Machine – page 81

Cut out the word strips along the green dotted lines. Do **not** cut the solid red line. Crease the strips along the solid red line. Place them unfolded in a bag.

Choose three students and have them stand in a line. Explain to the students that today they will put words through a silent E machine. Direct the first student to choose a word and read it. The second student should fold it. The third student will read it with the silent final E added.

LESSON 57

Objectives

SPELLING RULE: Review: The vowel says its long sound because of the E.

HANDWRITING: Learn uppercase ⬚K⬚ .

SPELLING: bike, nine, street, grape, high

Materials

NEEDED: LOE whiteboard, Tactile Card ⬚𝒦⬚ or ⬚K⬚ , Bingo game pieces, crayons or markers

OPTIONAL: Sidewalk chalk, Phonogram Game Tiles

Phonogram Practice

Phonogram Bingo

57.1 Phonogram Bingo – pages 83-34

Using the Bingo Game provided, call out sounds while the students cover them. Play until the board is covered. Direct the students to read the phonograms back as they uncover each square on the board.

Bingo game pieces such as pennies, crackers, or other small items to cover the squares

Spelling Rule Review

Silent E

In the last lesson we learned a new rule for when a vowel will say its long sound. I will write a word on the board. I want you to read it.

Write *tap*

> *tap*

Add an e: *tape*

> What does this say? *tape*

If the student reads *tape* correctly, then ask him,

Why does the vowel say its long sound in *tape*? *The vowel says its long sound because of the E.*

If the student misreads the word, cover up the silent E and say,

What does this say? *tap*

Then uncover the E and say,

What does this say? *tape*

Help the student sound it out if necessary.

57.2 Silent Final E – page 85

Crayons or markers

Now we will play a game. In your workbook, you have pairs of words. I will read one word of the words, and I want you to color in the correct word.

The first word is *cap*. Put the cap on the milk. *cap*
Which one should you color in? *The one without the silent E.*
Why? *Because with a silent E it would say cape.*

hat   bite
cane   note
rob

57.3 Silent Final E Challenge – page 86

Crayons or markers

Read the words aloud. Ask the student to color in the correct word.

paste
slid
plan
scrape

Handwriting

Writing Uppercase K

57.4 Uppercase K – page 87

Whiteboard
Tactile Card or K

Compare and contrast the upper- and lowercase /k/ in a bookface font and in the handwriting font.

Let's learn how to write the uppercase /k/.
Demonstrate how to write uppercase /k/ using K or K.

Start halfway between the mid-line and the top line. ①**Curve** up to the top line, ②**straight** to the baseline, ③pick up the pencil, start at the top line, ④**slash** down to the midline, ⑤**kick** down to the baseline.

Start at the top line. ①**Straight** to the baseline, ②pick up the pencil, ③start at the top line, ④**slash** to the midline, ⑤touch, ⑥**kick** down to the baseline.

Write uppercase /k/ three times on the Tactile Card or in the air, using your pointer finger.

Write uppercase /k/ three times on your whiteboard.
Which one looks most like the Tactile Card?
Put a smiley face next to the best /k/.

Multi-Sensory Fun

Practice writing the uppercase phonograms with sidewalk chalk.

Writing on Paper

57.4 Uppercase K – page 87

Write uppercase /k/ three times on your favorite line size.

Spelling

Spelling List

Teach the words using the steps for Spelling Analysis. Direct students to write the words on their whiteboards or with Phonogram Game Tiles.

Word	Sentence	Say to Spell	Markings	Spelling Hints
1. bike	*He rode his bike to the park.*	bīk	bīke	Put a line over the /ī/. Double underline the silent E. The vowel said its long sound because of the E. We could NOT use CK because CK is used only after a single, short vowel.
2. nine	*My brother is nine years old.*	nīn	nīne	Put a line over the /ī/. Double underline the silent E. The vowel said its long sound because of the E.
3. street	*The car is parked on the street.*	strēt	street	Underline E double E, which always says /ē/.
4. grape	*Grape juice is my favorite.*	grāp	grāpe	Put a line over the /ā/. Double underline the silent E. The vowel said its long sound because of the E.
5. high	*The balloon floated high into the sky.*	hī	high	Underline three letter /ī/. English words do not end in I, U, V, or J. Therefore, we cannot use single letter I at the end.

bike

The first word is *bike.* He rode his bike to the park. *bike*
How many syllables in *bike*? **one**
Let's sound it out. */b-ī-k/*
You will need a tall /k/.
What will we need to make the long /ī/ sound? **silent final E**
Now write *bike.* Sound it out as you write it. */b-ī-k/*
The student writes *bike* on his whiteboard.

It is now my turn to write *bike.* Sound it out as I write it. */b-ī-k/*
The teacher writes *bike* on the board.

Vocabulary

Discuss the meanings of *bike.*

The *bike* is in the garage.
I *bike* to school every day.

What does this say? */b-ī-k/ bike*

With your hand, cover up the Silent E.

Now what does it say? *bĭk*

Uncover the Silent E.

How will we mark a silent E? *Underline it twice.*

Why do we have a silent final E in bike? *to make the I say its long sound /ī/*

Since I said its long sound, draw a line over it.

Write *bicke* on the board.

Why can't we use two-letter /k/ to spell *bike*? *Because the I says its long sound. Two-letter /k/ is used only after a short vowel.*

nine

The second word is *nine*. My brother is nine years old. *nine*

How many syllables in *nine*? *one*

Let's sound it out. */n-ī-n/*

What will we need to make the long /ī/ sound? *silent final E*

Now write *nine*. Sound it out as you write it. */n-ī-n/*

The student writes *nine* on his whiteboard.

It is now my turn to write *nine*. Sound it out as I write it. */n-ī-n/*

The teacher writes *nine* on the board.

What does this say? */n-ī-n/ nine*

With your hand, cover up the Silent E.

Now what does it say? *nĭn*

Uncover the Silent E.

How will we mark a silent E? *Underline it twice.*

Why do we have a silent final E in nine? *to make the I say its long sound /ī/*

Since the phonogram I said its long sound, draw a line over it.

Reading

Find It!

57.5 Find It! – page 88

Read the word. Look at the picture. Find the object in the picture. Notice that some of the words end with a /s-z/. This means they are plural. When the word is plural, there will be more than one in the picture. Count how many you find and write the number in the blank.

LESSON 58

Objectives

PHONEMIC AWARENESS: Learn that U has two long vowel sounds.

SPELLING RULE: Review reading questions.

HANDWRITING: Learn uppercase $\boxed{\text{V}}$.

SPELLING: fire, cute, pick, flute, sheep

Materials

NEEDED: LOE whiteboard, Basic Phonogram Flash Card $\boxed{\text{u}}$, Tactile Card $\boxed{\mathcal{V}}$ or $\boxed{\text{V}}$, Phonogram Game Cards, stop watch, game pieces, scissors

OPTIONAL: Paper and pencil, Phonogram Game Tiles

Phonemic Awareness

Long U

Show the students the Phonogram Card $\boxed{\text{u}}$.

Basic Phonogram Flash Card $\boxed{\text{u}}$

What does this say? */ŭ-ū-ö-ü/.*
How many sounds is this? *four*
What is the short sound? */ŭ/*

Say /ū/. */ū/*
Now say /ö/. */ö/*

How are /ū/ and /ö/ the same? *They both say /ö/.*
How are they different? */ū/ has a /y/ sound at the beginning and /ö/ does not.*
/ö/ and /ū/ are related sounds. In fact they are BOTH the long sounds of U.

Sometimes we drop the /y/ sound so our tongues don't trip.

Write *cute* on the board.
What does this say? */k-ū-t/*

Write *flute* on the board.
What does this say? */f-l-ö-t/*

Now try to say /f-l-yö-t/. *f-l-yö-t*
Do you feel how your tongue trips on the /y/ sound? *yes*
Sometimes we drop the /y/ sound so our tongues do not trip. /ö/ is still a long sound.

Show the students the u .
What are the two long sounds? */ū/ and /ö/*

Handwriting

Writing Uppercase V

58.1 Uppercase V – page 89

Whiteboard
Tactile Card *V* or V

Compare and contrast the upper- and lowercase /v/ in a
bookface font and in the handwriting font.

Let's learn how to write the uppercase /v/.
Demonstrate how to write uppercase /v/ using *V* or V .

*Start halfway between the mid-
line and the top line.* [1]**Curve** up
to the top line, [2]**down** to the
baseline, [3]**swing** up to the top
line, [4]**dip** just below the top
line.

Start at the top line. [1]**Kick** down
to the baseline, [2]**angle up** to the
top line.

Write uppercase /v/ three times on the Tactile Card or in the air, using your pointer finger.
Write uppercase /v/ three times on your whiteboard.
Which one looks most like the Tactile Card?
Put a smiley face next to the best /v/.

Writing on Paper

58.1 Uppercase V – page 89

Write uppercase /v/ three times on your favorite line size.

LESSON 59

Objectives

PHONEMIC AWARENESS: Review the ways to make a vowel say its long sound.

SPELLING RULES: Silent E words.

HANDWRITING: Learn uppercase Y.

SPELLING: like, ride, keep, pink, quick

Materials

NEEDED: LOE whiteboard, Tactile Card Y or Y, two sets of Phonogram Game Cards, game board and words from worksheet 58.3, game pieces, scissors

OPTIONAL: Phonogram Game Tiles

Phonogram Practice

Phonogram Slap

Place the Phonogram Game Cards face up on the table, facing the students. Call out a phonogram's sound(s) and direct the students to race to slap the correct phonogram.

2 sets of Phonogram Game Cards

Classroom: Phonogram Slap

Divide students into groups of 2-4. Place the Phonogram Game Cards face up on the table, facing the students. Be sure that all the students can read the phonograms straight on. Call out a phonogram's sound(s) and direct the students to race to slap the correct phonogram. The first one to slap it takes it.

2 sets of Phonogram Game Cards for every 4 students

Teacher Tip

Be sure to have all students reading the phonograms in the upright position. Many young students will develop visual confusion issues when asked to read phonograms sideways or upside down across a table.

108

Handwriting

Writing Uppercase Y

59.1 Uppercase Y – page 95

Whiteboard
Tactile Card or Y

Compare and contrast the upper- and lowercase /y-ĭ-ī-ē/ in a bookface font and in the handwriting font.

Let's learn how to write the uppercase /y-ĭ-ī-ē/.
Demonstrate how to write uppercase /y-ĭ-ī-ē/ using   or Y .

Start halfway between the mid-line and the top line. ①**Curve** up to the top line, ②**down** to the baseline, ③**swing** up to the top line, ④**drop** down halfway below the baseline, ⑤**swoop.**

Start at the top line. ①**Kick** down to the midline, ②pick up the pencil, start at the top line, ③**slash** down to the baseline.

Write uppercase /y-ĭ-ī-ē/ three times on the Tactile Card or in the air, using your pointer finger.

Write uppercase /y-ĭ-ī-ē/ three times on your whiteboard.
Which one sits on the baseline the best?
Which one looks most like the Tactile Card?
Put a smiley face next to the best /y-ĭ-ī-ē/.

Writing on Paper

59.1 Uppercase Y – page 95

Write uppercase /y-ĭ-ī-ē/ three times on your favorite line size.

Phonemic Awareness

Long Vowel Sounds

What are two ways we have learned to make a long vowel sound in English? *A E O U usually say their long sounds at the end of the syllable. The vowel says its long sound because of the E.*

I will write a word on the board that has a long sound. Read the word. Then tell me why the vowel says its long sound. Each time you get it right, I will give you 1 point. When you reach 10 points you win!

she	store	mule
me	name	hike
lake	lane	maze
bake	so	wave
cute	tape	flute
go	cane	cave
tube	we	

59.2 Silent Final E – page 96

When we are spelling words, we need to listen and hear if the vowel is long or short. This helps us to know how to spell the vowel sound.

Look at the pictures. Decide if you need to add an E to make the vowel sound long, or if the word is spelled correctly without the silent final E.

Silent E Board Game

59.3 Silent E Game – pages 97-98

Cut out the words in your workbook and put the words face down in a pile. Put your game piece on start on the game board. Draw a word from the pile. If you read it correctly the first time, you may move two spaces. If you misread it, but then read it correctly the second time, you may move one space. If you misread it the second time, we will read it together, and then the card will go back into the pile.

Game Board and words from 58.3

Game pieces

Scissors

Multi-Sensory Fun

Save the words and game board to be used with Lesson 63. This is also an excellent game to save for further practice reading words that end with a silent final E.

Spelling

Spelling List

Teach the words using the steps for Spelling Analysis. Direct students to write the words on their whiteboards or with Phonogram Game Tiles.

Teacher Tip

Pink - In some dialects the vowel sound widens so that *pink* has a similar vowel sound to *peek*, while in other dialects, it is closer to the sound in *pin*. Emphasize the short /ĭ/ sound for spelling.

	Word	Sentence	Say to Spell	Markings	Spelling Hints
1.	like	*Do you like chocolate?*	līk	līk͟e͟	Put a line over the /ī/. Double underline the silent E. The vowel said its long sound because of the E. We could NOT use CK because CK is used only after a single, short vowel.
2.	ride	*He will ride the horse.*	rīd	rīd͟e͟	Put a line over the /ī/. Double underline the silent E. The vowel said its long sound because of the E.
3.	keep	*You may keep the change.*	kēp	k͟ee͟p	Underline E double E, which always says /ē/.
4.	pink	*Her favorite color is pink.*	pĭnk	pink	All first sounds.
5.	quick	*The girl with red hair is very quick.*	kwik	q͟u͟ick	Underline /kw/. Q always needs a U. U is not a vowel here. Underline two-letter /k/ which is used only after a single, short vowel.

Reading Practice

Silent E Matching

59.4 Matching – pages 99-100

Read the sentence. Match it to the correct picture.

Multi-Sensory Fun

Cut out the pictures and sentences. Put the sentences on one side of the room and the pictures on the other. Ask the students to choose a sentence, run to the other side of the room and find the picture, then place the match in a third spot.

Objectives

PHONEMIC AWARENESS: Change the inital sound to form new words.

PHONOGRAM: Learn ng .

HANDWRITING: Learn uppercase C .

SPELLING: thing, sing, clock, snake, note

READER 4

Materials

NEEDED: LOE whiteboard, Tactile Card 𝒞 or 𝒞 , Basic Phonogram Flash Card ng , Phonogram Game Tiles, Bingo game pieces, Reader 4

OPTIONAL: Crayons or markers, paper

Handwriting

Writing Uppercase C

60.1 Uppercase C – page 101

Compare and contrast the upper- and lowercase /k-s/ in a bookface font and in the handwriting font.

Let's learn how to write the uppercase /k-s/.
Demonstrate how to write uppercase /k-s/ using 𝒞 or 𝒞 .

Whiteboard
Tactile Card 𝒞 or 𝒞

Start halfway between the top line and the midline. [1]**Roll** around to just above the baseline.

Start just below the top line. [1]**Roll** around to just above the baseline.

Write uppercase /k-s/ three times on the Tactile Card or in the air, using your pointer finger.

Write uppercase /k-s/ three times on your whiteboard.

Which one sits on the baseline the best?

Which one touches the top line neatly?

Put a smiley face next to the best /k-s/.

Phonograms

The Phonogram ng

Show the Phonogram Card ng .

This says /ng/. What does it say? *Ing/*

Write /ng/ three times on your whiteboard.

Whiteboard

Basic Phonogram Flash Card ng

Teacher Tip

If students confuse /n/ and /ng/, help them develop a kinesthetic awareness of how the sounds are formed. Contrast words like *win* and *wing*, or *kin* and *king*.

Phonemic Awareness

Creating New Words

Today we will make new words using phonogram tiles. I have arranged the letters in a pattern. I want you to read the word I have created.

| s | i | ng |

What does this say? *sing*

What happens if I change the /s/ to /w/?

| w | i | ng |

What does this say? *wing*

If I add a /s/ to the beginning, now what will I have?

| s | w | i | ng |

What does this say? *swing*

If you trade the beginning letter(s), what new words can you form? *king, ding, ring, being, cling, bring, fling, sling, sting, thing*

If desired, make other words ending in NG: bang, fang, gang, hang, sang, hung, lung, clung, flung, bong, dong, gong, song, long.

Phonogram Game Tiles

60.2 The Phonogram NG – page 102

Look at each picture and say the word out loud. Listen to the first sound(s). Fill in the blank to complete the word.

Phonogram Practice

Phonogram Bingo

60.3 Phonogram Bingo – pages 103-104

Bingo game pieces, such as pennies, crackers, or other small items

Using the Bingo Game provided, call out sounds while the students cover them. Play until the board is covered.
Direct the students to read the phonograms back as they uncover each square on the board.

Spelling

Spelling List

Teach the words using the steps for Spelling Analysis. Direct students to write the words on their whiteboards or with Phonogram Game Tiles.

	Word	Sentence	Say to Spell	Markings	Spelling Hints
1.	thing	*What is that thing?*	thĭng	thing	Underline /th/. Underline /ng/.
2.	sing	*I love to sing.*	sĭng	sing	Underline /ng/.
3.	clock	*My alarm clock is by my bed.*	klŏk	clock	Underline two-letter /ck/, used only after a single, short vowel.
4.	snake	*The snake slithered across the path.*	snāk	snāke	Put a line over the /ā/. Double underline the silent E. The vowel said its long sound because of the E. We could NOT use CK because CK is used only after a single, short vowel.
5.	note	*My mom wrote me a note.*	nōt	nōte	Put a line over the /ō/. Double underline the silent E. The vowel said its long sound because of the E.

Reading

Reader

Take out Reader 4. Ask the student to read the title and each page aloud.

When the student has finished the book, ask:

   What does Pete want? *a pet*

   Which picture is your favorite one in the book? Why? *Answers will vary.*

   How does this picture relate to the story? *Answers will vary.*

   Which pet would you pick and why?

Reader 4
Crayons or markers
Paper

Challenge

Ask students to write a story titled *The Pet Store*. Encourage them to draw pictures and to write words for each illustration. Provide feedback on spelling using the rules and phonograms. If the student desires to write a word which uses a phonogram that has not been taught, simply explain why it is spelled in that manner.

Multi-Sensory Fun

Ask the students to draw a picture of a pet they would pick and label it.

REVIEW D

Area	Skill	Mastery
Phonemic Awareness	Identify the long sounds of U.	2
	Change the initial sound to form a new word.	1
Handwriting	Write uppercase R, W, U, I, J.	2
	Write uppercase K, V, Y, C.	2
Phonograms	Read er, wh, oi, oy, ai, ay.	1
	Read ng.	2
Reading	Read and comprehend simple questions.	2
	Read words with a silent E which makes the vowel long.	2

Skills with a 1 should be mastered before students move on to the next lesson. For skills marked with a 2, students should demonstrate familiarity but not necessarily answer all the questions correctly. These skills will be practiced extensively in the upcoming lessons.

Phonemic Awareness Assessment

Long U

Basic Phonogram Flash Card u

Show the Phonogram Card u .
> What does this say? /ŭ-ū-ö-ü/
> What does the short sound say? /ŭ/
> What does the long sound say? /ū/ *and* /ö/

Initial Sounds

D.1 Initial Sounds – page 105

Look at the picture and say the word. Write the sound that you hear at the beginning of the word.

Handwriting Assessment

Handwriting

D.2 Handwriting – page 106

Write one of each phonogram on your favorite line size.

Multi-Sensory Fun

If the student is not ready to write on paper, show the student the phonogram card and have him write the phonogram on a whiteboard or in a sensory box.

Phonogram Assessment

Phonogram Assessment

Ask the student to read each of the following phonogram cards: er, wh, oi, oy, ai, ay, ng

Basic Phonogram Flash Cards er
wh oi oy ai ay ng

What's That Phonogram?

Highlighter

D.3 What's That Phonogram? – pages 107-108

On your page are groups of four phonograms. I will say a phonogram's sound(s). Color the phonogram with your highlighter.

1. /wh/
2. /oi/ that you may NOT use at the end of English words.
3. /ā/ two-letter /ā/ that you may NOT use at the end of English words.
4. /oy/ that you may use at the end of English words.
5. /ng/
6. /ā/ two-letter /ā/ that you may use at the end of English words.
7. /er/ the /er/ of her

Reading Assessment

Reading

D.4 Reading – pages 109-110

Read the question. Then read the answer. Circle the correct picture.

Practice Ideas

Initial Sounds

"Creating New Words" on page 40 in the Teacher's Manual
"Creating New Words" on page 113

Handwriting

Using the Tactile Cards, reteach how to write any of the phonograms which are difficult. Break down each step and have the student repeat the short, bold directions aloud.

"Optional Blind Writing" on page 40
"Phonogram Baseball" on page 54
"Phonogram Challenge" on page 75

Teacher Tip

Students who struggle with handwriting should practice writing using large motor movements. It is also beneficial for these students to recite the bold, rhythmic directions aloud when writing.

Phonograms

"Go Fish" on page 67

"Timed Phonogram Reading" on page 72

"Last One!" on page 82

"Phonogram Boat Race" on page 86

"Speed Writing" on page 106

"Phonogram Slap" on page 108

"Phonogram Bingo" on page 114

Silent Final E's

Teacher Tip

Quickly reteach the first reason for a silent final E. Write the following words on the board.

Read each word as I write it on the board.

Choose activities to practice as needed. Go back to previous lessons and reteach concepts that need more practice.

cap	*cut*
rip	*pet*
not	

Then add a silent E to each word. Mark the long vowel and the silent E.

Now I will change the word. Read the new word to me.

cape	*cute*
ripe	*Pete*
note	

Why did the vowel become long? *The vowel says its long sound because of the E.*

Practice reading silent final E words with the follow games.

"Silent Final E" on page 95

"Silent E Machine" on page 98

"Silent E Board Game" on page 107

Objectives

PHONEMIC AWARENESS: Listen for silent final E's.

SPELLING RULE: English words do not end in V.

HANDWRITING: Learn uppercase $\boxed{E}$.

SPELLING: have, give, smile, ask, thank

Materials

NEEDED: LOE whiteboard, Tactile Card $\boxed{\mathcal{E}}$ or $\boxed{E}$, two sets of Phonogram Game Cards, Basic Phonogram Flash Card $\boxed{v}$, scissors, glue, prizes for store

OPTIONAL: Phonogram Game Tiles, window paint

Handwriting

Writing Uppercase $\boxed{E}$

61.1 Uppercase E – page 111

Whiteboard
Tactile Card $\boxed{\mathcal{E}}$ or $\boxed{E}$

Compare and contrast the upper- and lowercase /ĕ-ē/ in a bookface font and in the handwriting font.

Let's learn how to write the uppercase /ĕ-ē/.
Demonstrate how to write uppercase /ĕ-ē/ using $\boxed{\mathcal{E}}$ or $\boxed{E}$.

Start halfway between the top line and the midline. ①**Roll** around to the midline, ②**roll** around to just above the baseline.

Start at the top line. ①**Straight** to the baseline, ②pick up the pencil, ③**cross** at the top line, ④pick up the pencil, ⑤**cross** at the midline, ⑥pick up the pencil, ⑦**cross** at the baseline.

Write uppercase /ĕ-ē/ three times on the Tactile Card or in the air, using your pointer finger.

Write uppercase /ĕ-ē/ three times on your whiteboard.

Which one sits on the baseline the best?

Which one looks most like the Tactile Card?

Put a smiley face next to the best /ĕ-ē/.

Writing on Paper

61.1 Uppercase E – page 111

Write uppercase /ĕ-ē/ three times on your favorite line size.

61.2 Match the Sound – page 112

I will read a phonogram. Circle all the ways that phonogram is written.

1. /ĕ-ē/
2. /y-ĭ-ī-ē/
3. /j/
4. /ĭ-ī-ē-y/
5. /m/
6. /r/

Phonogram Game

Phonogram Memory

Choose phonograms that need further review.

Mix the Phonogram Game Cards. Lay all the cards face down in rows in the middle of the table. The first player chooses a card and flips it upright so everyone may see. He reads the sounds. The player then chooses a second card, flips it upright, and reads the sounds. If the phonograms match, he keeps the pair and goes again. If the phonograms do not match, he flips them back to face down and play passes to the next player. Play ends when all the pieces are matched. The player with the most sets wins.

2 sets of Phonogram Game Cards in different colors

Multi-Sensory Fun

Use window paint and write the phonograms on a window or mirror.

Phonemic Awareness

Listening for Silent Final E's

61.3 Silent E's – pages 113-116

We have learned that one way to make a vowel say its long sound is to add a silent final E. Look at the picture. Say the word.

Which pictures will need a silent final E at the end? *kite, hive, cake, bike, rake, rope*

Cut out the words. Read each word and glue it below the correct picture.

Scissors
Glue

Challenge

Look at the picture, then write the word in the blank. Listen for a long vowel.

Spelling Rule

VE

Show the Phonogram Card ⊡ v ⊡.

Basic Phonogram Flash Card ⊡ v ⊡

What does this say? */v/*
What is the name of this letter? *V*
Do we know a rule about V? *English words do not end in I, U, V, or J.*

Today I need you to be a spelling detective again. I have a problem and I need your help to figure it out. Let's write the word *have*. You sound it out as I write it on the whiteboard. */h-ă-v/*

Write *hav* on the board.

Hmm. It ends in the sound /v/. But English words cannot end in V. Do you have any guesses about how I can solve this problem? *answers will vary*
I will solve it by adding a silent final E.

Add the E to make *have.*

Why do we need an E in the word *have*? *English words do not end in V.*
Does the silent E make the vowel say its long sound /ā/? *No, it doesn't say /h-ā-v/. It is there because English words do not end in V.*

Here is another word. What does this say?

Write *give* on the board.

/g-ĭ-v/ give
Why do we need a silent final E in *give*? *English words do not end in V.*

Write *cave* on the board.

Does /căv/ make sense? *no*

What does this say? *cave*

Why do we need a silent final E in cave? *It makes the A says its long sound /ā/, AND English words do not end in V.*

There are two reasons for the silent E. Whenever you see a silent final E in a word, you always need to ask, "Why do I need the E?"

Spelling

Spelling List

Teach the words using the steps for Spelling Analysis. Direct students to write the words on their whiteboards or with Phonogram Game Tiles.

Word	Sentence	Say to Spell	Markings	Spelling Hints
1. have	*They have a red car.*	hăv	ha<u>ve</u>	Underline the silent E twice. Underline the V once. English words do not end in V; add a silent final E.
2. give	*Mom will give you a lunch.*	gĭv	gi<u>ve</u>	Underline the silent E twice. Underline the V once. English words do not end in V; add a silent final E.
3. smile	*She has a beautiful smile.*	smɪl	smī<u>le</u>	Put a line over the /ī/. Double underline the silent E. The vowel said its long sound because of the E.
4. ask	*Did you ask a question?*	ăsk	ask	All first sounds.
5. thank	*Thank you for the gift.*	thănk	<u>th</u>ank	Underline /th/.

have

The first word is *have*. They have a red car. *have*

Place your hand under your chin and say, "have." How many syllables in *have*? *have, one*

Let's sound it out. */h-ă-v/*

What will you need at the end? *silent final E*

Why? *English words do not end in V.*

Now write *have.* Sound it out as you write it.   /h-ă-v/

The student writes *have* on his whiteboard.

It is now my turn to write *have.* Sound it out as I write it.   /h-ă-v/

The teacher writes *have* on the board.

What does this say?   /h-ă-v/   *have*

With your hand cover up the Silent E.

Now what does it say?   /h-ă-v/

So why do we need a Silent Final E?   *English words do not end in V.*

Uncover the Silent E.

How will we mark a silent E?   *underline it twice*

Why do we have a silent final E in *have*?   *for the V*

Since we need the E for the V, we will underline the V once. This will help us to remember why we needed the E.

give

The second word is *give.* Mom will give you a lunch. *give*

Place your hand under your chin and say, "give." How many syllables in *give*?   *give, one*

Let's sound it out.   /g-ĭ-v/

What will you need at the end?   *silent final E*

Why?   *English words do not end in V.*

Now write *give.* Sound it out as you write it.   /g-ĭ-v/

The student writes *give* on his whiteboard.

It is now my turn to write *give.* Sound it out as I write it.   /g-ĭ-v/

The teacher writes *give* on the board.

What does this say?   /g-ĭ-v/   *give*

With your hand cover up the Silent E.

Now what does it say?   /g-ĭ-v/

So why do we need a silent final E?   *English words do not end in V.*

Uncover the Silent E.

How will we mark a silent E?   *underline it twice*

Why do we have a silent final E in *give*?   *for the V*

Since we need the E for the V, we will underline the V once. This will help us to remember why we needed the E.

Reading Practice

Silent E Store

Decide on a price for each type of prize. Begin with the lowest prize around 10 points and the highest prize around 50 points. A class may collectively play for 50-75 points to earn a collective prize such as an extra 5 minutes of recess or a small snack.

3-4 options for prizes (crackers, raisins, ice cream bar, ball, pencil)

Today, I will write a word on the board. If you read it correctly, you receive one point. If there is a silent final E and you tell me why it is needed, you receive one point for each reason you explain correctly. You may buy a prize when you have enough points or you may save up points for a bigger prize.

dive	ship	fish
cub	live	pin
cube	fire	wave
have	plane	band
toy	say	boy
cute	gate	drum
sock	prune	her
tape	fat	plain
sing	hive	wing
kite	same	right
flat	sale	spit
tap	coin	stone
play	he	mule
time	five	rule
give	trick	bike
base	drove	rock
when	and	way
bone	sleep	wish
flute	sight	came
she	brave	past
store	cave	paste
night	spot	wife
cone	tune	home
truck	rat	stick
thing	day	line
flame	pine	

Objectives

PHONEMIC AWARENESS: Review the long sounds of U.

SPELLING RULE: English words do not end in U.

HANDWRITING: Learn uppercase O .

SPELLING: blue, true, must, save, game

Materials

NEEDED: LOE whiteboard, Tactile Card or 𝒪 , Basic Phonogram Flash Card u , two sets of Phonogram Game Cards

OPTIONAL: Phonogram Game Tiles, scissors

Handwriting

Writing Uppercase O

Whiteboard
Tactile Card 𝒪 or 𝒪

62.1 Uppercase O – page 117

Compare and contrast the upper- and lowercase /ŏ-ō-ö/ in a bookface font and in the handwriting font.

Let's learn how to write the uppercase /ŏ-ō-ö/.
Demonstrate how to write uppercase /ŏ-ō-ö/ using 𝒪 or 𝒪 .

 Start at the top line. ①**Roll** around past the baseline and back up to the top line, ②**swirl**.

 Start just below the top line. ①**Roll** around past the baseline, back up to the top line.

Write uppercase /ŏ-ō-ö/ three times on the Tactile Card or in the air, using your pointer finger.

Write uppercase /ŏ-ō-ö/ three times on your whiteboard.
Which one sits on the baseline the best?
Which one looks most like the Tactile Card?

Put a smiley face next to the best /ŏ-ō-ö/.

Writing on Paper

62.1 Uppercase O – page 117

Write uppercase /ŏ-ō-ö/ three times on your favorite line size.

Phonemic Awareness

Long U

Show the students the ⬚ u .

What does this say? */ŭ-ū-ö-ü/.*

What is the short sound? */ŭ/*

How many long sounds does U have? *two*

What are the long sounds? */ū/ and /ö/*

Basic Phonogram Flash Card ⬚ u

I will say a word with a sound of U. Stretch your arms out straight like a line if it is a long sound. Hold them over your head in a curve if it is a short sound.

blue *long*	tune *long*	true *long*
cute *long*	hunt *short*	much *short*
cut *short*	fume *long*	clue *long*

Spelling Rule

English Words Do Not End in U

Today I need you to be a spelling detective again.

Let's sound out the word *clue*. You sound it out as I write it on the whiteboard. */k-l-ö/*

Write *clu* on the board.

Let's read it. */k-l-ö/*

Why is the U saying its long sound? *It is at the end of the syllable. A E O U usually say their long sounds at the end of the syllable.*

What is wrong with this? *It ends in a U. English words do not end in I, U, V, or J.*

What do you think I should do about it? *Add a silent final E.*

Add the E to make *clue*.

Does the silent E make the vowel say its long sound /ö/? *No, it already says its long sound at the end of the syllable.*

Why do we need the silent final E? *English words do not end in U.*

Here is another word. What does this say?

Write *true* on the board.

/t-r-ö/ *true*

Why do we need a silent final E in *true*? *English words do not end in U.*

This is our new reason for a silent final E. We say, "English words do not end in V or U." Let's say that together. *English words do not end in V or U.*

What is the other reason we have learned for a silent final E? *The vowel says its long sound because of the E.*

Let's memorize our new silent final E rule together: *English words do not end in V or U.*

Let's say the rule in a silly voice: *English words do not end in V or U.*

Let's whisper the rule: *English words do not end in V or U.*

Phonogram Practice

Dragon

Mix two sets of Phonogram Game Cards together. Deal out all the cards to the players. Some players may have one more or one less card than others. Players should hold their cards in a fan in their hand. Players look through their hand and lay down any matches. As they lay down a match, they must read the sounds. To begin play, the first player chooses another player from whom to draw a card. If he draws a card that matches one in his hand, the sound(s) are read, the match is laid down, and the player takes another turn. If a match is not found, the player adds the new card to his hand. Play then moves to the next player on the left. Play ends when someone lays down all his cards. The player left holding the Dragon card loses.

2 sets of 20-30 Phonogram Game Cards
learned in previous lessons
1 Dragon card

Spelling

Spelling List

Teach the words using the steps for Spelling Analysis. Direct students to write the words on their whiteboards or with Phonogram Game Tiles.

Word	Sentence	Say to Spell	Markings	Spelling Hints
1. blue	*The team will wear blue shirts.*	blö	blue	Underline the silent final E twice. Underline the U once. English words do not end in V or U; add a silent final E.
2. true	*Is that story true?*	trö	true	Underline the silent final E twice. Underline the U once. English words do not end in V or U; add a silent final E.
3. must	*We must go to bed early tonight.*	mŭst	must	All first sounds.
4. save	*I save pennies.*	sāv	sāve	Put a line over the /ā/. Double underline the silent E. The vowel said its long sound because of the E. Underline the V once. English words do not end in V or U; add a silent final E.
5. game	*That is my favorite game.*	gām	gāme	Put a line over the /ā/. Double underline the silent E. The vowel said its long sound because of the E.

save

The next word is *save*. I save pennies. *save*
Place your hand under your chin and say, "save." How many syllables in *save*? **save, one**
Let's sound it out. */s-ā-v/*
What will you need at the end? **silent final E**
Why do we need a silent final E? **We need it for two reasons: English words do not end in V, and to make the A say its long sound /ā/.**
Now write *save*. Sound it out as you write it. */s-ā-v/*
The student writes *save* on his whiteboard.

It is now my turn to write *save*. Sound it out as I write it.   */s-ā-v/*

The teacher writes *save* on the board.

What does this say? */s-ā-v/ save*

With your hand, cover up the Silent E.

Now what does it say? */s-ă-v/*

Why do we need a silent final E? *The E makes the A say its long sound /ā/, and English words do not end in V.*

How many reasons are there for a silent final E in *save*? *two*

How will we mark this word? *Draw a line over the A because it said its long sound. Underline the V because it is one of the reasons for the E. Underline the E twice because it is silent.*

Reading Practice

Matching

62.2 Matching – pages 118-119

Read the sentence. Match it to the correct picture.

Scissors

Multi-Sensory Fun

Cut out the pictures and sentences. Put the sentences on one side of the room and the pictures on the other. Ask the students to choose a sentence, run to the other side of the room and find the picture, then place the match in a third place.

Objectives

PHONEMIC AWARENESS: Review how to spell Silent Final E words.

HANDWRITING: Learn uppercase ⟨Q⟩.

SPELLING: take, wave, song, drive, glue

Materials

NEEDED: LOE whiteboard, Tactile Card ⟨𝒬⟩ or ⟨𝒬⟩, sidewalk chalk or paper plates and markers, Basic Phonogram Flash Cards, beanbag or stone, scissors

OPTIONAL: Phonogram Game Tiles

Handwriting

Writing Uppercase ⟨Q⟩

63.1 Uppercase Q – page 120

Compare and contrast the upper- and lowercase /kw/ in a bookface font and in the handwriting font.

Let's learn how to write the uppercase /kw/.
Demonstrate how to write uppercase /kw/ using ⟨𝒬⟩ or ⟨𝒬⟩.

Whiteboard
Tactile Card ⟨𝒬⟩ or ⟨𝒬⟩

Start at the baseline. ①**Circle** around past the top line to the baseline, ②**loop** on the baseline.

Start just below the top line. ①**Roll** around past the baseline back up to the top line, ②pick up the pencil, start just inside the circle, ③**kick** out to the baseline.

131

Write uppercase /kw/ three times on the Tactile Card or in the air, using your pointer finger.

Write uppercase /kw/ three times on your whiteboard.
Which one sits on the baseline the best?
Which one looks most like the Tactile Card?
Put a smiley face next to the best /kw/.

Writing on Paper

63.1 Uppercase Q – page 120

Write uppercase /kw/ three times on your favorite line size.

Phonogram Practice

Phonogram Hopscotch

Draw a hopscotch board without anything in the squares. Show the student a Phonogram Card. Have him read it, then write it in the square of his choice. Fill in all the squares in this manner. Direct the student to toss a beanbag onto one of the squares. He then hops to the beanbag, reading each phonogram he passes, picks up the beanbag, and hops back again reading each of the sounds.

Sidewalk chalk
10-20 Basic Phonogram Flash Cards for sounds that need review
Beanbag or stone to toss

Indoor Phonogram Hopscotch

Provide the student with a paper plate. Show the student a Phonogram Card. Have her read it, then write the phonogram on the plate. Continue until all the review phonograms have been used. Use the paper plates to play Phonogram Hopscotch. (In a classroom have all the students create a set.)

Paper plates
Markers
10-20 Basic Phonogram Flash Cards for sounds that need review
Beanbag or stone to toss

Classroom: Phonogram Relay

Divide students into teams of 2-4 students. Each team should set out one set of Phonogram Plates on the floor. Each team then lines up behind their plates. When the teacher says, "go," the first student should hop onto each plate and read the sound(s).When he reaches the end, he turns around, runs back, and tags the next person in line.

Write phonograms that need review on 10-20 paper plates per team

Silent Final E's

Correct the Teacher

There are a few words I have forgotten how to spell. Will you help me?

The first word is *have*. I will sound it out and write it. You need to tell me if there is anything wrong. /h-ă-v/

Write *hav*.

Is this correct? *No, you need a silent final E.*

Why? *English words do not end in V.*

Add the E to write *have*.

The next word is *cape*. /k-ā-p/

Write *cap*.

Is this correct? *No, you need a silent final E.*

Why? *It says cap. You need a silent final E to make the vowel sound long.*

Add the E to write *cape*.

The next word is *map*. /m-ă-p/

Write *mape*.

Is this correct? *No, you do not need a silent final E.*

Why? *It would say māp.*

Take off the E to spell *map*.

The next word is *clue*. /k-l-ö/

Write *clu*.

Is this correct? *No, you need a silent final E.*

Why? *English words do not end in V or U.*

Add the E to write *clue*.

Teacher Tip

/ö/ represents the sound found in the words *do, shoe, and clue.*

If desired, continue with:

rip	flute	cute
not	solve	due
crave	zone	cut
pet	save	jet

Spelling

Spelling List

Teach the words using the steps for Spelling Analysis. Direct students to write the words on their whiteboards or with Phonogram Game Tiles.

	Word	Sentence	Say to Spell	Markings	Spelling Hints
1.	take	*Did you take your coat?*	tāk	tāk<u>e</u>	Put a line over the /ā/. Double underline the silent E. The vowel said its long sound because of the E.
2.	wave	*Wave your hand and say goodbye.*	wāv	wā<u>ve</u>	Put a line over the /ā/. Double underline the silent E. The vowel said its long sound because of the E. Underline the V once. English words do not end in V or U.
3.	song	*That is my favorite song.*	sŏng	so<u>ng</u>	Underline the /ng/.
4.	drive	*It will be a long drive to Florida.*	drīv	drī<u>ve</u>	Put a line over the /ī/. Double underline the silent E. The vowel said its long sound because of the E. Underline the V once. English words do not end in V or U.
5.	glue	*This glue dries quickly.*	glö	gl<u>ue</u>	Underline the silent final E twice. Underline the U once. English words do not end in V or U.

Reading

High Frequency Word Charades

Scissors

63.2 Charades – pages 121-122

Cut out the words. Place them upside down in a pile. Ask the student to choose a word, read it silently, then act it out. Guess the word.

Teacher Tip

Save the High Frequency Word Cards for use with other word games.

Objectives

PHONEMIC AWARENESS: Learn to rhyme words.

PHONOGRAM: Learn ar .

HANDWRITING: Learn uppercase G .

SPELLING: car, far, same, jar, ring

Materials

NEEDED: LOE whiteboard, Basic Phonogram Flash Card ar , two sets of Phonogram Game Cards, timer, cloth bag, Tactile Card 𝒢 or 𝒢 , scissors

OPTIONAL: Phonogram Game Tiles

Phonograms

The Phonogram ar

Show the Phonogram Card ar .
> This says /ar/. What does it say? **/ar/**
> Write /ar/ three times on your whiteboard.

Whiteboard
Basic Phonogram Flash Card ar

Speech Tip

Some children struggle to articulate the sound /ar/. Begin by asking the student to say /r/. Ask the child to feel where his tongue is and how it is touching the sides of his teeth. Then ask the student to say /ä/. Feel how the mouth is open and the tongue is relaxed. Ask the student to say /ä/ then /r/, feeling his tongue and mouth. Then slowly blend the two sounds together.

Phonogram Practice

Rotten Egg

Place all the Phonogram Game Cards in the bag with the *Rotten Egg* card(s). Set the timer for an undisclosed time of 1-3 minutes. Students* take turns drawing a card and reading the phonogram aloud. If they get it right, they keep the card and pass the bag to the next player. If they do not read the phonogram correctly, they must put it back in the bag and pass the bag to the next person. If a student draws a *Rotten Egg* card, he must put all his cards back in the bag and pass it to the next player. Play ends when the timer beeps. The student holding the most cards wins.

*Rotten Egg may be played with one student and a teacher.

2 sets of Phonogram Game Cards
1-2 Rotten Egg cards
Timer
Cloth bag
Snatch It! card

Multi-Sensory Fun

Add a Snatch It! card to the bag. If a student draws the Snatch It! card, she may take the cards of any other player.

Handwriting

Writing Uppercase G

64.1 Uppercase G – page 123

Compare and contrast the upper- and lowercase /g-j/ in a bookface font and in the handwriting font.

Let's learn how to write the uppercase /g-j/.
Demonstrate how to write uppercase /g-j/ using or G .

Whiteboard
Tactile Card  or G

Start at the baseline. ①**Loop** up to the top line, ②**down** to the midline, ③**swing** up to halfway between the midline and the top line, ④**scoop** around past the baseline, ⑤**glide** across.

Start just below the top line. ①**Roll** around past the baseline to the midline, ②**draw** a line straight into the circle.

Write uppercase /g-j/ three times on the Tactile Card or in the air, using your pointer finger.

Write uppercase /g-j/ three times on your whiteboard.
Which one sits on the baseline the best?
Which one looks most like the Tactile Card?
Put a smiley face next to the best /g-j/.

Writing on Paper

64.1 Uppercase G – page 123

Write uppercase /g-j/ three times on your favorite line size.

Phonemic Awareness

Rhymes

Today we will learn how to rhyme words. I will say two words that rhyme. I want you to tell me what you notice about the words.

hat   cat
They both end in -at.

Here are two more words that rhyme. What do you notice about them?

fold   hold
They both end in -old

I will say two words. If they rhyme, stand up and shout "yes!" If they do not rhyme, sit down and shake your head, "no."

cold	told	*yes*		tree	hip	*no*
less	yes	*yes*		sad	lamp	*no*
had	look	*no*		sad	dad	*yes*
had	mad	*yes*		lamp	ramp	*yes*
look	book	*yes*				

64.2 Rhyming – pages 124-125

Read the word. Look at the pictures. Circle the ones that rhyme with the word.

Teacher Tip

Many children with weak auditory skills struggle with rhyming. Rhyming requires students to break the word into sounds, isolate the final vowel and consonant sound and compare those sounds to another word. Rhyming skills are not needed to become fluent readers and spellers.

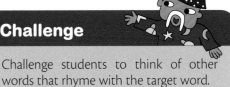

Challenge

Challenge students to think of other words that rhyme with the target word.

Spelling

Spelling List

Teach the words using the steps for Spelling Analysis. Direct students to write the words on their whiteboards or with Phonogram Game Tiles.

	Word	Sentence	Say to Spell	Markings	Spelling Hints
1.	car	*My car is parked in back.*	kar	c<u>ar</u>	Underline /ar/.
2.	far	*How far did you run today?*	far	f<u>ar</u>	Underline /ar/.
3.	same	*They are wearing the same shirt.*	sām	sām<u>e</u>	Put a line over the /ā/. Double underline the silent E. The vowel said its long sound because of the E.
4.	jar	*Pass the jar of jam.*	jar	j<u>ar</u>	Underline /ar/.
5.	ring	*Did you hear my phone ring?*	rĭng	ri<u>ng</u>	Underline /ng/.

Reading

Ben's Fun Day

64.3 Ben's Fun Day – pages 126-127

Cut out the pictures.
Then you will read about Ben's Fun Day. After you read each sentence, find the picture that describes what Ben is doing and show it to me.

Scissors

Teacher Tip

In a classroom, ask the students to read the sentence quietly, choose the picture, then hold it up to show you.

Multi-Sensory Fun

Play a memory game with the pictures and sentences about Ben's Fun Day. Cut out the sentences and the pictures. Place all the pictures and sentences face down on the table. Ask the student to choose one sentence and one picture. Read the sentence. If they match, he may keep them both and go again. If they do not match, he must flip them over and wait for another turn, or try again.

Objectives

PHONEMIC AWARENESS: Practice rhyming words.

PHONOGRAM: Learn or .

SPELLING: or, for, much, gave, sight

READER 5

Materials

NEEDED: LOE whiteboard, Basic Phonogram Flash Card or , Bingo tokens such as raisins or pennies, Reader 5. For cursive only: Tactile Cards 𝓂, 𝒶, 𝓇, 𝒸, ℊ, 𝓆, 𝓊

OPTIONAL: Phonogram Game Tiles, toy cars

Phonograms

The Phonogram or

Show the Phonogram Card or .

Whiteboard
Basic Phonogram Flash Card or

This says /or/. What does it say? **/or/**
Write /or/ three times on your whiteboard.

Phonogram Practice

Phonogram Bingo

Bingo tokens such as raisins or pennies

65.1 Phonogram Bingo – pages 129-130

Using the Bingo Game provided, call out sounds while
the students cover them. Play until the board is covered. Direct the students to read the
phonograms back as they uncover each square on the board.

Phonemic Awareness

Rhyme

Today we will practice rhyming again. I will say two words that rhyme. I want you to see if you can think of a third word that rhymes with them.

cat	hat	*bat, sat, mat, fat, rat*
flop	hop	*top, pop, stop, mop, cop*
ball	call	*fall, wall, tall, mall, crawl, small*
thing	swing	*ring, sing, wing, bring, spring, fling, string*
go	low	*hoe, sew, toe, know, glow, show, slow, mow, row, blow*

65.2 Rhyming – page 131

Read the word. Find the picture that rhymes. Draw a line to it.

Toy cars

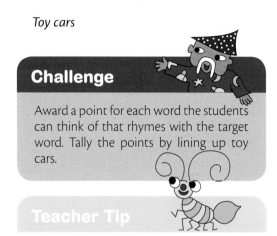

Challenge

Award a point for each word the students can think of that rhymes with the target word. Tally the points by lining up toy cars.

Teacher Tip

Notice that words which rhyme may be spelled using a variety of phonograms. This is because some vowels have multiple ways to spell the same sound in English.

Spelling

Spelling List

Teach the words using the steps for Spelling Analysis. Direct students to write the words on their whiteboards or with Phonogram Game Tiles.

Word	Sentence	Say to Spell	Markings	Spelling Hints
1. or	*Would you like one or two pieces?*	or	<u>or</u>	Underline the phonogram /or/.
2. for	*This is for you.*	for	f<u>or</u>	Underline /or/.
3. much	*How much does it cost?*	mŭch	mu<u>ch</u>	Underline /ch/.
4. gave	*Dad gave me ten dollars.*	gāv	gā<u>ve</u>	Put a line over the /ā/. Double underline the silent E. The vowel said its long sound because of the E. Underline the V once. English words do not end in V or U; add a silent final E.
5. sight	*That was an amazing sight.*	sīt	<u>sight</u>	Underline three-letter /ī/.

Handwriting

Connecting Cursive Uppercase Letters

The main purpose of this exercise is to introduce the concept of connecting uppercase cursive letters in words. The students do not need to master it at this time. Cursive uppercase letters that do not connect to the next letter will be introduced in lesson 68.

Tactile Cards $\mathcal{M}$, $\mathcal{A}$, $\mathcal{R}$, $\mathcal{C}$, $\mathcal{J}$, $\mathcal{Q}$, $\mathcal{U}$

Cursive only

Now we will learn how to write words with uppercase letters. Do you remember where we use uppercase letters? *Answers will vary.*

We use uppercase letters at the beginning of a sentence and for names.

When we write a word, where do we normally pick up our pencil? *at the end of the word*

What happens between the letters in a word? *They are connected.*

Show tactile cards for uppercase $\mathcal{M}$, $\mathcal{A}$, $\mathcal{R}$, $\mathcal{C}$, $\mathcal{J}$, $\mathcal{Q}$, $\mathcal{U}$.

Where does each of these letters end? *at the baseline*

These letters connect to the next letter in the word. Let's try it together. I will show you, and then you try it on your whiteboard.

Write *Mom*, saying the strokes as you write. Repeat with *Jack* and *Queen*. Have the students practice with their whiteboards, saying the strokes as they write.

Reading

Reader

Take out Reader 5. Ask the student to read each page aloud.

When the student has finished the book, ask:

What did you notice about Jake's farm?

What is personification? *When animals or objects act like people.*

Were any of the animals personified in this story? *yes*

How? *The hens knit, the pig can ride a donkey, and the cats sing songs.*

What is your favorite part of the story?

Reader 5

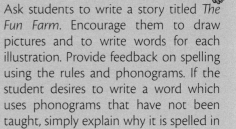

Challenge

Ask students to write a story titled *The Fun Farm*. Encourage them to draw pictures and to write words for each illustration. Provide feedback on spelling using the rules and phonograms. If the student desires to write a word which uses phonograms that have not been taught, simply explain why it is spelled in that manner.

REVIEW E

Area	Skill	Mastery
Phonemic Awareness	Determine if a word needs a silent final E for the vowel.	2
	Rhyme words.	3
Handwriting	Write uppercase K, V, Y, C.	2
	Write uppercase E, O, Q, G.	2
Phonograms	Read ng.	1
	Read ar, or.	2
Reading	Read and comprehend simple sentences.	2
	Read words with silent final E's.	2

Skills with a 1 should be mastered before students move on to the next lesson. For skills marked with a 2, students should demonstrate familiarity but not necessarily answer all the questions correctly. These skills will be practiced extensively in the upcoming lessons. Skills with a 3 do not need to be mastered in order for students to move on.

Phonemic Awareness Assessment

Silent Final E's

Highlighter

E.1 Silent Final E's – page 132

I will say a word. Highlight the correct spelling.

tape   globe

rate   cut

bit

Handwriting Assessment

Handwriting

E.2 Handwriting – page 133

Write one of each phonogram on your favorite line size

Multi-Sensory Fun

If the student is not ready to write on paper, show the student the phonogram card and have him write the phonogram on a whiteboard or in a sensory box.

Phonogram Assessment

Phonogram Assessment

Ask the student to read each of the following phonogram cards: ng, ar, or.

Basic Phonogram Flash Cards | ng |
| ar | or |

What's That Phonogram?

Highlighter

E.3 What's That Phonogram? – page 134

On your page are groups of four phonograms. I will say a phonogram's sound(s). Color the phonogram with your highlighter.

1. /or/
2. /ng/
3. /är/

Reading Assessment

Reading

E.4 Matching – pages 135-136

Read the sentence. Match it to the correct picture.

Practice Ideas

Initial Sounds

"Creating New Words" on page 40 in the Teacher's Manual
"Creating New Words" on page 113

Handwriting

Using the Tactile Cards, reteach how to write any of the phonograms which are difficult. Break down each step and have the student repeat the short, bold directions aloud.

"Optional Blind Writing" on page 40
"Phonogram Baseball" on page 54
"Phonogram Challenge" on page 75

Teacher Tip

Students who struggle with handwriting should practice writing using large motor movements. It is also beneficial for these students to recite the bold, rhythmic directions aloud when writing.

Phonograms

"Go Fish" on page 67
"Timed Phonogram Reading" on page 72
"Last One!" on page 82
"Phonogram Boat Race" on page 86
"Speed Writing" on page 106
"Phonogram Slap" on page 108
"Phonogram Bingo" on page 114

Silent Final E's

Quickly reteach the two reasons for a silent final E. Write
the following words on the board.

Read each word as I write it on the board.

cap	*cut*
rip	*pet*
not	

Now I will change the word. Read the new word to me.

Add a silent E to each word. Mark the long vowel and the silent E.

cape	*cute*
ripe	*Pete*
note	

Why did the vowel become long? *The vowel says its long sound because of the E.*

Practice reading silent final E words with the follow games.

"Silent Final E" on page 95
"Silent E Machine" on page 98
"Silent E Board Game" on page 107

Objectives

PHONEMIC AWARENESS: Learn about broad vowel sounds.

HANDWRITING: Learn uppercase L .

SPELLING: want, wash, to, snail, cave

Materials

NEEDED: LOE whiteboard, Tactile Card 𝓛 or 𝓔 , sensory box filled with sand, Basic Phonogram Flash Cards a , e , o , u , High Frequency Word Cards from Lessons 42, 48, 51, and 63, scissors, empty ice cream bucket

OPTIONAL: Phonogram Game Tiles, tray with shaving cream or whipped cream, construction paper and stickers, book from book list, story about a fox who raids a henhouse

Handwriting

Writing Uppercase L

66.1 Uppercase L – page 137

Compare and contrast the upper- and lowercase /l/ in a bookface font and in the handwriting font.

Let's learn how to write the uppercase /l/.
Demonstrate how to write uppercase /l/ using 𝓛 or 𝓔 .

Whiteboard
Tactile Card 𝓛 or 𝓔

Start halfway between the midline and the top line. ①**Glide** up to the top line, ②**roll**, ③**slash** down to the baseline, ④**loop** on the baseline.

Start at the top line. ①**Straight** to the baseline, ②**cross** at the baseline.

Write uppercase /l/ three times on the Tactile Card or in the air, using your pointer finger.

Write uppercase /l/ three times on your whiteboard.
Which one looks most like the Tactile Card?
Put a smiley face next to the best /l/.

Book List

Bob Books Set 1
Lad and the Fat Cat

Writing on Paper

66.1 Uppercase L – page 137

Write uppercase /l/ three times on your favorite line size.

Phonogram Practice

Sensory Writing

Explain to students that you will say a phonogram's sound(s). Using their pointer finger, the students should write the phonogram in the sand or cream.

Sensory box filled with sand
or tray with shaving cream or whipped cream

Phonemic Awareness

Broad Vowels

Show the phonogram a .

Basic Phonogram Flash Cards a , e , o , and u

What is the short sound of A? */ă/*
How do we mark the short sound? *Put a curved line (a breve) over it.*
Write ă on the board.

What is the long sound of A? */ā/*
How do we mark the long sound? *Put a straight line over it.*
Write ā on the board.

Show the phonogram a .

But how many sounds does A make? */ă-ā-ä/, three*
The third sound /ä/ is called the broad sound. We mark the broad sound with two dots.
Write ä on the board.

Place the phonograms e , o , and u where everyone can see them.

Which of these phonograms make more than two sounds? */ŏ-ō-ö/ and /ŭ-ū-ö-ü/*

Show the phonogram o .

What does this phonogram say? */ŏ-ō-ö/*
What is the first sound /ŏ/ called? *short*
How do we mark it? *with a curved line*

Write ŏ on the board.

What is the second sound /ō/ called? *long*
How do we mark it? *with a straight line*

Write ō on the board.

What is the third sound /ö/ called? *broad*
How do we mark it? *with two dots*

Write ö on the board.

Today we will learn more about broad vowels in words.

Show the phonogram u .

What does this phonogram say? */ŭ-ū-ö-ü/*
What is the first sound /ŭ/ called? *short*
How do we mark it? *with a curved line*

Write ŭ on the board.

What is the second sound /ū/ called? *long*
How do we mark it? *with a straight line*

Write ū on the board.

What is the third sound /ö/ called? *long*
How do we mark it? *with a straight line*

Write ū on the board.

What do you think the fourth sound /ü/ is called? *the broad sound*
How do we mark it? *with two dots*

Write ü on the board.

Today we will learn some words with broad vowels.

Spelling

Spelling List

Teach the words using the steps for Spelling Analysis. Direct students to write the words on their whiteboards or with Phonogram Game Tiles.

	Word	Sentence	Say to Spell	Markings	Spelling Hints
1.	want	*I want to play basketball.*	wänt	wänt	Put two dots over the /ä/. /ă-ā-ä/ said its broad sound. /ă-ā-ä/ may say its broad sound after a W.
2.	wash	*Did you wash your hands?*	wäsh	wä<u>sh</u>	Put two dots over the /ä/. /ă-ā-ä/ said its broad sound. /ă-ā-ä/ may say its broad sound after a W. Underline /sh/.
3.	to	*She gave the box to me.*	tö	tö	Put two dots over the /ŏ-ō-ö/. /ŏ-ō-ö/ said its broad sound.
4.	snail	*The snail crawled up the tree trunk.*	snāl	sn<u>ai</u>l	Underline two-letter /ā/. Two-letter /ā/ that may NOT be used at the end of English words.
5.	cave	*The tour group explored the cave.*	cāv	cā<u>ve</u>	Put a line over /ā/. Double underline the silent final E. The /ā/ said its long sound because of the E. Underline the V. English words do not end in V.

want

The first word is *want.* I want to play basketball. *want*
Place your hand under your chin and say, "want." How many syllables in *want*? ***want, one***
Let's sound it out. */w-ä-n-t/*
Now write *want.* Use /ă-ā-ä/ to spell the sound /ä/.
The student writes *want* on his whiteboard.

It is now my turn to write *want.* Sound it out as I write it.
/w-ä-n-t/
The teacher writes *want* on the board.

Teacher Tip

In some dialects /ä/ and /ŏ/ are pronounced as the same sound. Be sure to cue which phonogram to use when dictating a word that uses this sound. This is modeled for you in the scripting for *want* and *wash.*

What does this say? /w-ä-n-t/ *want*

What sound of /ă-ā-ä/ do you hear in *want*? *the broad sound /ä/*

How will we mark the broad sound? *Put two dots over it.*

/ă-ā-ä/ may say its broad sound after a W. In *want*, /ă-ā-ä/ came after a W, and it said its broad sound.

Teacher Tip

A may say its broad sound after a W. Students will learn more about this spelling rule in Foundations C. For reading, they simply need to understand that this is one of the sounds of the phonogram A.

wash

The next word is *wash*. Did you wash your hands? *wash*

Place your hand under your chin and say, "wash." How many syllables in *wash*? **wash, one**

Let's sound it out. /w-ä-sh/

Now write *wash*. Use /ă-ā-ä/ to spell the sound /ä/.

The student writes *wash* on his whiteboard.

It is now my turn to write *wash*. Sound it out as I write it.

/w-ä-sh/

The teacher writes *wash* on the board.

What does this say? /w-ä-sh/ *wash*

What sound of /ă-ā-ä/ do you hear in *wash*? *the broad sound /ä/*

How will we mark the broad sound? *put two dots over it*

/ă-ā-ä/ may say its broad sound after a W. In *wash*, /ă-ā-ä/ came after a W, and it said its broad sound.

to

The next word is *to*. She gave the box to me. *to*

Place your hand under your chin and say, "to." How many syllables in *to*? **to, one**

Let's sound it out. /t-ö/

How do we spell /ö/? *with /ŏ-ō-ö/*

The student writes *to* on his whiteboard.

It is now my turn to write *to*. Sound it out as I write it. /t-ö/

The teacher writes *to* on the board.

What does this say? /t-ö/ *to*

What sound of /ŏ-ō-ö/ do you hear in *to*? *the broad sound /ö/*

How will we mark the broad sound? *put two dots over it*

When you look at the word *to*, what do you expect it to say? *tō*

Why? *A E O U usually say their long sounds at the end of the syllable.*

Listen to the rule again. Notice if the rule says ALWAYS.

A E O U USUALLY say their long sounds at the end of the syllable. *No, it says USUALLY!*

Does usually mean always? *no*

If the vowel is not saying its long sound, it will be saying its broad sound. But what does it USUALLY say?

its long sound

Fox in the Hen House

66.2 Fox in the Hen House – pages 139-140

Cut out the words and place them in an ice cream bucket. Cut out the fox cards and mix them into the bucket. Tell each student to draw a word from the bucket. If she reads it correctly, she may keep it. If she does not, it goes back in the bucket. If she draws a fox card, the fox steals her cards and they all must go back in the bucket.

Variation: For faster game play, have the student put back five cards when the fox is drawn, or once the fox is drawn, put it aside.

Empty ice cream bucket

High Frequency Word Cards from
    Lessons 42, 48, 51, and 63

Scissors

Teacher Tip

Fox in the Hen House is a fun game that will repeat throughout the week with a new element to the game each day. It is highly recommended that teachers add in the high frequency words from lessons 42, 48, 51, and 63. It is also suggested that words that the student has mastered be pulled out of the game as the week progresses. Laminate the High Frequency Word Cards for durability, and save them in the word bucket. Lessons 66-70 place a strong emphasis on developing fluency with 148 of the 294 high frequency words taught in Foundations Level B.

Teacher Tip

Research demonstrates that students who read high frequency words without hesitation are able to focus greater attention on reading comprehension. Logic of English® takes a unique approach to high frequency words in that we do NOT teach these words as sight words. Rather, we teach students how to decode each word. The high frequency words are then practiced through fun games and activities until the student is able to decode the word "instantaneously."

Multi-Sensory Fun

Have the students decorate the ice cream bucket with construction paper and stickers. Read to your students a story about a fox who raids a henhouse.

Objectives

PHONEMIC AWARENESS: Explore the broad /ü/ sound.

SPELLING RULE: We often double F, L and S after a single vowel at the end of a base word.

HANDWRITING: Learn uppercase $\boxed{\text{X}}$.

SPELLING: put, off, stuff, star, chair

Materials

NEEDED: LOE whiteboard, Phonogram Game Cards, Basic Phonogram Flash Card $\boxed{\text{u}}$, matchbox cars, Tactile Card $\boxed{\mathcal{X}}$ or $\boxed{\mathcal{X}}$, scissors, word bucket, High Frequency Word Cards from Lessons 42, 48, 51, 63, 66

OPTIONAL: Phonogram Game Tiles, window paint, index cards, book from book list

Phonogram Slap

Place the Phonogram Game Cards face up on the table, facing the students. Call out a phonogram's sound(s) and direct the students to race to slap the correct phonogram.

15-20 Phonogram Game Cards

Classroom: Phonogram Slap

Divide students into groups of two to four. Be sure that all the students can read the phonograms straight on. Call out a phonogram's sound(s). Students may race to slap the phonogram. The first one to slap it takes it.

15-20 Phonogram Game Cards per group of 4 students

Phonemic Awareness

Broad U

Show the Phonogram Card u .

What does this say? */ŭ-ū-ö-ü/*

How many sounds is that? Let's say the sounds and count them together. */ŭ-ū-ö-ü/ four sounds*

The last sound /ü/ is the broad sound.
I will say a sound. You tell me if it is the short or the broad sound of /ŭ-ū-ö-ü/.

/ü/ *broad*
/ŭ/ *short*
/ŭ/ *short*
/ü/ *broad*

How do we mark the broad sound? **with two dots**

Write ü on the board.

Let's practice reading a few words where U says /ü/. I will write words on the board. Each time you read a word correctly, you may zoom one car across the floor or the desk.

pull

put

Now I will mix up words that use the first sound of U, /ŭ/, and the last sound of U, /ü/. Try the first sound /ŭ/. If that does not make sense, try the last sound /ü/. When you read it correctly, you may zoom a car across the floor or the desk.

push	*ü*		bus	*ŭ*
pull	*ü*		tub	*ŭ*
put	*ü*		full	*ü*

Basic Phonogram Flash Card  u

Matchbox cars
Window paint
Index cards

Teacher Tip

The short sound, /ŭ/, is the vowel sound in *puppy* and *up*. The broad sound, /ü/, can be heard in *pudding* and *put*.

Multi-Sensory Fun

Write the words on index cards. Stand them up in the crack of a table. Zoom the car at the word once it has been read correctly.

Handwriting

Writing Uppercase X

67.1 Uppercase X – page 141

Compare and contrast the upper- and lowercase /ks-z/ in a

Whiteboard
Tactile Card 𝒳 or 𝒳

bookface font and in the handwriting font.

Let's learn how to write the uppercase /ks-z/.
Demonstrate how to write uppercase /ks-z/ using or 𝒳 .

Start halfway between the mid-line and the top line. ①**Curve** up to the top line, ②**kick** down to the baseline, ③pick up the pencil, start at the top line, ④**slash** down to the baseline.

Start at the top line. ①**Kick** down to the baseline, ②pick up the pencil, start at the top line, ③**slash** down to the baseline.

Write uppercase /ks-z/ three times on the Tactile Card or in the air, using your pointer finger.

Write uppercase /ks-z/ three times on your whiteboard.
Which one sits on the baseline the best?
Which one looks most like the Tactile Card?
Put a smiley face next to the best /ks-z/.

Writing on Paper

67.1 Uppercase X – page 141

Write uppercase /ks-z/ three times on your favorite line size.

Spelling Rule

Double F

67.2 Spelling Mystery – page 142

Today you will be a spelling detective. On your page you have a list of words. I want you to read each word. There is something the same about all the words. When you find what is the same, raise your hand.

There are two F's at the end of the word.

Often if there is a /f/ at the end of the word, and there is a one-letter vowel, we will write two F's. This leads to our new spelling rule: We often double F, L, and S after a single vowel at the end of a base word.

Say the rule with me. *We often double F, L, and S after a single vowel at the end of a base word.*
Let's shout the rule. *We often double F, L, and S after a single vowel at the end of a base word.*
Let's whisper the rule. *We often double F, L, and S after a single vowel at the end of a base word.*

Spelling

Spelling List

Teach the words for students to write on their whiteboards. Use the steps for Spelling Analysis.

Word	Sentence	Say to Spell	Markings	Spelling Hints
1. put	*Where did you put your coat?*	püt	püt	Put two dots over the /ü/. /ŭ-ū-ö-ü/ said its broad sound.
2. off	*Please turn off the light.*	ŏf	off	We often double F, L, and S after a single vowel at the end of a base word.
3. stuff	*I brought too much stuff.*	stŭf	stuff	We often double F, L, and S after a single vowel at the end of a base word.
4. star	*The star is twinkling.*	star	st<u>ar</u>	Underline the /ar/.
5. chair	*The black chair is saved for him.*	chār	<u>ch</u><u>ai</u>r	Underline /ch/. Underline two-letter /ā/.

put

The first word is *put.* Where did you put your coat? *put*
Place your hand under your chin and say, "put." How many syllables in *put*? ***put, one***
Let's sound it out. */p-ü-t/*
How do you spell /ü/? ***Use /ŭ-ū-ö-ü/.***
The student writes *put* on his whiteboard.

It is now my turn to write *put.* Sound it out as I write it. */p-ü-t/*
The teacher writes *put* on the board.
What does this say? */p-ü-t/ put*
What sound of /ŭ-ū-ö-ü/ do you hear in *put*? ***the /ü/ sound or the broad sound***
How will we mark the broad sound? ***Put two dots over it.***

off

The next word is *off.* Please turn off the light. *off*
Place your hand under your chin and say, "off." How many syllables in *off*? ***off, one***
Let's sound it out. */ŏ-f-f/*
How many /f/s? ***two***

The student writes *off* on his whiteboard.

It is now my turn to write *off*. Sound it out as I write it. */ŏ-f-f/*

The teacher writes *off* on the board.

What does this say? */ŏ-f-f/ off*

Why did we double the F? **It is at the end of the word, and there is a single vowel. We often double F, L, and S after a single vowel at the end of a base word.**

stuff

The next word is *stuff*. I brought too much stuff. *stuff*

Place your hand under your chin and say, "stuff." How many syllables in *stuff*? **stuff, one**

Let's sound it out. */s-t-ŭ-f-f/*

How many /f/s? **two**

The student writes *stuff* on his whiteboard.

It is now my turn to write *stuff*. Sound it out as I write it.
/s-t-ŭ-f-f/

The teacher writes *stuff* on the board.

What does this say? */s-t-ŭ-f-f/ stuff*

Why did we double the F? **We often double F, L, and S after a single vowel at the end of a base word.**

Teacher Tip

As the student sounds out *stuff*, add a second /f/ sound: /s-t-ŭ-f-f/. This helps students create an auditory picture of the word.

Book List

Bob Books Set 1
    Muff and Ruff

Fluency

Fox in the Hen House

67.3 Fox in the Hen House – pages 143-144

Cut out the words and the number cards and add them to the Word Bucket. Tell each student to draw a word from the bucket. If she reads it correctly, she may keep it. If she does not, it goes back in the bucket. If she draws a fox card, the fox steals her cards and they all must go back in the bucket. If she draws a number card, she may draw that many extra cards. Each one she reads correctly, she may keep.

Scissors

Word Bucket with cards from Lessons
    42, 48, 51, 63, 66

Teacher Tip

Remove words that the student reads quickly. Use the game to practice developing fluency on words that the student is still audibly sounding out. The goal is for the student to read the word so quickly that it appears to be instantaneous. Studies have shown that students who master reading the high frequency words are able to focus more on reading comprehension. Laminate the High Frequency Word Cards for repeated use.

Objectives

PHONEMIC AWARENESS: Practice short, long, and broad vowels.

SPELLING RULE: We often double F, L and S after a single vowel at the end of a base word.

HANDWRITING: Learn uppercase Z .

SPELLING: ball, tall, do, tray, trail

Materials

NEEDED: LOE whiteboard, Tactile Card *Z* or Z , Basic Phonogram Flash Cards, raisins or tokens for Bingo, timer, scissors, word bucket, Fox cards and Number cards from previous lessons. Cursive only: all uppercase tactile cards.

OPTIONAL: Phonogram Game Tiles, balance beam or masking tape

Handwriting

Writing Uppercase Z

68.1 Uppercase Z – page 145

Whiteboard
Tactile Card *Z* or Z
Cursive only: uppercase Tactile Cards

Compare and contrast the upper- and lowercase /z/ in a bookface font and in the handwriting font.

Let's learn how to write the uppercase /z/.
Demonstrate how to write uppercase /z/ using *Z* or Z .

Start halfway between the midline and the top line. ①**Curve** up to the top line, ②**tuck** down to the baseline, ③**drop** down halfway below the baseline, ④**swoop**.

Start at the top line. ①**Cross** at the top line, ②**slash** down to the baseline, ③**cross** at the baseline.

158

Write uppercase /z/ three times on the Tactile Card or in the air, using your pointer finger.

Write uppercase /z/ three times on your whiteboard.
Which one sits on the baseline the best?
Which one looks most like the Tactile Card?
Put a smiley face next to the best /z/.

Writing on Paper

68.1 Uppercase Z – page 145

Write uppercase /z/ three times on your favorite line size.

Connecting Cursive Uppercase Letters in Words

Cursive only: Did you notice where uppercase /z/ ends? *at the baseline*

Show tactile cards for uppercase $\boxed{a}$, $\boxed{R}$, $\boxed{Q}$.
  Where do these letters end? *at the baseline*
  How do we write these letters in a word? *We connect them to the next letter.*

Show tactile cards for uppercase $\boxed{V}$, $\boxed{W}$, $\boxed{T}$, $\boxed{O}$, $\boxed{P}$, $\boxed{D}$.
  Do you see a problem with these? *They don't end on the baseline. It is hard to connect them.*
  That is right. When we write these letters, we will not connect them. We will write the uppercase letter right next to the other letters in the word to show that they are part of the same word. I will show you, and then you can try it on your whiteboard.

Write *Dad,* saying the strokes as you write. Repeat with *Pete.*
  When you write an uppercase letter that ends on the base line in a word, what will you do? *connect it*
  When you write an uppercase letter that does NOT end on the base line in a word, what will you do? *I will not connect it.*

Provide the students with the tactile cards $\boxed{m}$, $\boxed{a}$, $\boxed{R}$, $\boxed{C}$, $\boxed{g}$, $\boxed{Q}$, $\boxed{U}$, $\boxed{V}$, $\boxed{W}$, $\boxed{T}$, $\boxed{O}$, $\boxed{P}$, $\boxed{D}$. Ask them to sort them into uppercase letters that connect to the next letter and uppercase letters that do not connect to the next letter.

Phonogram Practice

Phonogram Tight Rope

Direct the student to stand against the wall. Show him a phonogram. Ask him to read the sounds. If he reads it

15-20 Basic Phonogram Cards to review
Balance beam or masking tape

correctly, he may take one step forward. His heel must touch his toe for each step. Then he should write the phonogram in the air. If he writes it correctly he may take another step. When he reaches (choose a location), he wins the game.

Multi-Sensory Fun

Use a balance beam, or put tape on the floor to make a line to balance on.

Classroom: Phonogram Stop and Go

Choose one student to be the "Stop and Go Light," holding a set of all the Phonogram Cards that have been learned so far. Line up the remaining students side by side in a line facing the "Stop and Go Light." When the student with the Phonogram Cards turns his back to the students, they must remain still. The "Stop and Go Light" announces how the students will move forward. For example: tiptoe, baby steps, giant steps… The "Stop and Go Light" turns around showing a phonogram. The students read all the sounds. For each sound, they can take one step forward. The "Stop and Go Light" turns back around, chooses the next phonogram, and announces how they will move forward. When the students reach the "Stop and Go Light," a new student is chosen to lead.

Basic Phonogram Flash Cards

Phonemic Awareness

Vowel Bingo

68.2 Vowel Bingo – page 146

I will say a sound. Cover it up on your Bingo card.

Call out the sounds until all the squares have been covered.

/ō/	/ĭ/
/ŏ/ - /ä/	/ū/ - /ö/
/ĕ/	/ā/
/ă/	/ö/
/ü/	/ŭ/
/ē/	

Raisins or tokens for Bingo

Timer

Teacher Tip

Short /ŏ/ and broad /ä/ sound the same in many dialects. If your students hear them as the same, alert them to to cover two squares when you say this sound.

Now, read the sounds on the Bingo card to me as quickly as you can in the direction of reading and writing. I will time you.

/ä/	/ō/	/ū/ - /ö/
/ē/	/ĭ/	/ŏ/
/ā/	/ö/	/ü/
/ĕ/	/ŭ/	/ă/

Try a second time. Do you think you can beat your time?

Spelling Rule

Double L

Scissors

68.3 Spelling Mystery – pages 147-148

Cut out the cards and hide them around the room.

Today you need to be a detective. I have hidden mystery words or clues around the room. First you will need to search for a clue. When you find the clue, read it. Then find the next clue and read it. You need to find the pattern in these words and see if you can figure out which rule describes these words.

There are two L's at the end of each word. We often double F, L, and S after a single vowel at the end of a base word.

Do we always? *No, we often do.*

Let's say the rule loudly. *We often double F, L, and S after a single vowel at the end of a base word.*

Spelling

Spelling List

Teach the words for students to write on their whiteboards. Use the steps for Spelling Analysis.

	Word	Sentence	Say to Spell	Markings	Spelling Hints
1.	ball	*The ball bounced across the gym.*	bäl	bäll	Put two dots over the /ä/. /ă-ā-ä/ said its broad sound. We often double F, L, and S after a single vowel at the end of a base word.
2.	tall	*How tall are you?*	täl	täll	Put two dots over the /ä/. /ă-ā-ä/ said its broad sound. We often double F, L, and S after a single vowel at the end of a base word.
3.	do	*What should we do?*	dö	dö	Put two dots over the /ö/. /ŏ-ō-ö/ said its broad sound.
4.	tray	*The tray has two cups on it.*	trā	tr<u>ay</u>	Underline two-letter /ā/. Two-letter /ā/ that may be used at the end of English words.
5.	trail	*The trail is two hundred miles long.*	trāl	tr<u>ai</u>l	Underline two-letter /ā/. Two-letter /ā/ that may NOT be used at the end of English words.

Fluency

Fox in the Hen House

68.4 Fox in the Hen House – pages 149-150

Cut out the new words and the trap cards and add them to the Word Bucket. Tell each student in turn to draw a word from the bucket. If she reads it correctly, she may keep it. If she does not, it goes back in the bucket. If she draws a fox card, the fox steals her cards and they all must go back in the bucket. If she draws a number card, she may draw that many extra cards. Each one she reads correctly, she may keep. If she draws the trap card, she may use it to trap the fox. (In other words, she keeps the trap card and she will not need to give up her cards if she draws the fox on her turn.)

Scissors

Word Bucket

Fox cards and Number cards from previous lessons

Teacher Tip

A list of the high frequency words taught in Foundations B is available on page VI in the introduction. They are listed in the order in which they are introduced, beginning with the first column from top to bottom.

Objectives

PHONEMIC AWARENESS: Practice short, long, and broad vowels.

SPELLING RULE: We often double F, L and S after a single vowel at the end of a base word.

SPELLING: class, mess, short, pull, shall

Materials

NEEDED: LOE whiteboard, markers or crayons, finger paint and paper, highlighter, scissors, word bucket, Fox, Number and Trap cards, High Frequency Word Cards from Lessons 42, 48, 51, 63, 66-68, timer. Cursive only: Uppercase Tactile Cards

OPTIONAL: Phonogram Game Tiles

Phonemic Awareness

Long, Short, and Broad Vowels

Markers or crayons

69.1 Long, Short, and Broad Vowels – page 151

On your page you have a list of vowels with their markings.
Read the sounds to me.

Now, I will say a color and read you a sound. As I read the sounds, circle them with the crayon color that I say.

red /ĕ/
blue /ä/ and /ŏ/ Notice there is a short and a broad vowel that both say /ŏ/
orange /ā/
green /ö/
black /ē/
brown /ă/

Phonogram Practice

Finger Painting

Practice writing the phonograms with the pointer finger using finger paint. Practice writing it with the thumb, pinkie finger, etc. Make it fun!

Finger paint
Paper

Spelling Rule

Double S

Highlighter

69.2 Spelling Mystery – page 152

Today I want you to be a Word Detective again. On your worksheet you have a list of words. You need to read the words aloud and then highlight what is the same about every word. When you know what is the same, raise your hand.

mess	moss	glass
less	toss	grass
miss		

There are two S's at the end of each word.

What other letters do we double at the end of the word? *F, L*
We often double F, L, and S after a single vowel at the end of a base word.
Do we always? *No, we often do.*
Let's say the rule together with a silly voice. *We often double F, L, and S after a single vowel at the end of a base word.*

Spelling

Spelling List

Teach the words using the steps for Spelling Analysis. Direct students to write the words on their whiteboards or with Phonogram Game Tiles.

	Word	Sentence	Say to Spell	Markings	Spelling Hints
1.	class	*What time does class start?*	klăs	class	We often double F, L, and S after a single vowel at the end of a base word.
2.	mess	*Let's clean up the mess.*	mĕs	mess	We often double F, L, and S after a single vowel at the end of a base word.
3.	short	*I am very short.*	short	sh<u>or</u>t	Underline /sh/. Underline /or/.
4.	pull	*Pull the rope as hard as you can.*	pül	püll	Put two dots over the /ü/. U said its broad sound. We often double F, L, and S after a single vowel at the end of a base word.
5.	shall	*Shall we have dinner now?*	shăl	<u>sh</u>all	Underline /sh/. We often double F, L, and S after a single vowel at the end of a base word.

Fluency

Fox in the Hen House

69.3 Fox in the Hen House – pages 153-154

Cut out the new words and the timer card and add them to the Word Bucket.

Scissors
Word Bucket
Fox cards, Number cards, and Trap cards
Timer

Tell each student to draw a word from the bucket. If she reads it correctly, she may keep it. If she does not, it goes back in the bucket. If she draws a fox card, the fox steals her cards and they all must go back in the bucket. If she draws a number card, she draws that many extra cards. Each one she reads correctly, she may keep. If she draws the trap card, she may use it to trap the fox. (In other words, she will not need to give up her cards if she draws the fox on her turn.) If she draws the timer, set a timer for 10-15 seconds. The student must then read as many cards as possible during that time. She keeps all the cards she reads correctly. (The fox card does not count during a timer session.)

Handwriting

Using Uppercase Letters

Cursive Tactile Cards - uppercase

Cursive Only

Do you remember what we learned about writing uppercase letters in words? *If an uppercase letter ends on the baseline, we connect it with the whole word. If it does not end on the baseline, we do not connect it.*

Show

Does uppercase /t/ end on the baseline? *No. It is near it, but not on it. We don't connect it.*

Give students an assortment of uppercase cursive tactile cards. Have them practice sorting them into letters that do connect to the next letter and letters that don't.

Manuscript Only

When you read a sentence in a book, what kind of letter does it start with? *An uppercase letter*
What kind of letter will we use when we write a sentence? *An uppercase letter*
Do you remember where else we use uppercase letters? *Answers will vary*
We use uppercase letters at the beginning of a sentence and for a name.

Handwriting Practice

69.4 Handwriting – page 155

Students now know how to write all the lowercase and uppercase letters. An optional handwriting worksheet will be provided each lesson for students to practice. Ask the student to read the sentence aloud before writing it on her favorite line size.

> **Teacher Tip**
>
> If your student is progressing more slowly in handwriting than in reading or is not yet ready to write on paper, do not worry. Provide handwriting practice at whatever level is comfortable for the student, focusing on large motor movements.

Reading

Reading Comprehension

69.5 The Ball Game – page 156-157

The soccer team is making plans for how to practice passing the ball. Read the directions. Draw a line from player to player to show how the ball will move.

Objectives

PHONEMIC AWARENESS: Practice rhyming words.

SPELLING RULE: We often double F, L and S after a single vowel at the end of a base word. Occasionally other letters also are doubled.

SPELLING: egg, buzz, bring, cake, way

READER 6

Materials

NEEDED: LOE whiteboard, scissors, two sets of Phonogram Game Cards, word bucket, Fox, Number, Trap, and Timer cards from previous lessons, timer, Reader 6

OPTIONAL: Phonogram Game Tiles

Phonemic Awareness

Rhyming

I will say two words that rhyme. Then I want you to think of a third word that rhymes with them.

tall	hall	*ball, mall, wall, call, fall*
hit	bit	*lit, mitt, sit, pit, kit, fit, knit*
cat	sat	*mat, hat, pat, rat, fat*

70.1 Rhyming – page 158-159

Find the words on the page that rhyme. Draw a line between them.

Handwriting

Handwriting Practice

70.2 Handwriting – page 160

Handwriting sheets are optional. Ask the student to read the sentence aloud before writing it. If the student does not have adequate fine motor development to write the sentence on the worksheet, the student may also write the sentence on his whiteboard.

Challenge

Dictate the sentence aloud for the student to write on a separate sheet of paper or on her whiteboard.

Spelling Rule

Other Double Letters

Scissors

70.3 Spelling Mystery – pages 161-162

Cut out the cards and hide them around the room.

Today we have a very tricky spelling mystery. I have again hidden clues around the room. This time you do not know the whole rule. I want you to gather the clues. Read them. When you think you know the solution to the mystery, then come and whisper it to me.

All of the words end in double letters.
What is the rule we learned? *We often double F, L, and S...*
Do any of these words end in an F, L, or S? *no*
There is a bit more to the rule. We often double F, L, and S after a single vowel at the end of a base word. Occasionally other letters also are doubled.

What does occasionally mean? *Answers will vary.*
Let me give you some examples of it in a sentence.
Occasionally I eat fish, but not very often.
Occasionally we go to the movie theater, but not very often.

What does occasionally mean? *not very often*
What do you do occasionally? *Answers will vary.*
So if we occasionally double other letters, do we do it very often? *no*

Let's say the rule together in a loud voice. *We often double F, L, and S after a single vowel at the end of a base word. Occasionally other letters also are doubled.*

Phonogram Practice

Phonogram Memory

Mix the Phonogram Game Cards. Lay all the cards face down in rows in the middle of the table. The first player chooses a card and flips it upright so everyone may see it, and reads the sound(s). He then chooses a second card, flips it upright, and reads the sounds. If the phonograms match, he keeps the pair and goes again. If the phonograms do not match, he returns them to the rows face down and play passes to the next player. The game ends when all the pieces are matched. The player with the most phonogram pairs wins.

2 sets of 20 Phonogram Game Cards in different colors

Spelling

Spelling List

Teach the words using the steps for Spelling Analysis. Direct students to write the words on their whiteboards or with Phonogram Game Tiles.

	Word	Sentence	Say to Spell	Markings	Spelling Hints
1.	egg	*The egg is dyed pink and green.*	ĕg	egg	We often double F, L, and S after a single vowel at the end of a base word. Occasionally other letters also are doubled.
2.	buzz	*Did you hear the alarm buzz?*	bŭz	buzz	We often double F, L, and S after a single vowel at the end of a base word. Occasionally other letters also are doubled.
3.	bring	*Bring your coat.*	brĭng	bri<u>ng</u>	Underline /ng/.
4.	cake	*She brought a birthday cake.*	kāk	cāk<u>e</u>	Put a line over the /ā/. Double underline the silent final E. The /ā/ said its long sound because of the E.
5.	way	*Which way did they go?*	wā	w<u>ay</u>	Underline two letter /ā/. English words do not end in I, U, V, or J. Therefore we cannot use AI. When a word ends in a single-letter A it usually says /ā/.

Fluency

Fox in the Hen House

70.4 Fox in the Hen House – page 163-164

Cut out the new words and add them to the Word Bucket. Tell each student to draw a word from the bucket. If she reads it correctly, she may keep it. If she does not, it goes back in the bucket. If she draws a fox card, the fox steals her cards and they all must go back in the bucket. If she draws a number card, she may draw that many extra cards. Each one she reads correctly, she may keep. If she draws the trap card, she may use it to trap the fox. (In other words, she will not need to give up her cards if she draws the fox on her turn.) If she draws the timer, set a timer for 10-15 seconds. The student must then read as many cards as possible during that time. She may keep all the cards she reads correctly. (The fox card does not count during a timer session.) If a student draws "Put Back 2 Cards" she must put two cards back into the bucket.

Scissors
Word Bucket
Fox cards, Number cards, Trap cards and
    Timer cards from previous lessons
Timer

Teacher Tip

Save the Word Bucket and cards for use in Lesson 77.

Reading

Reader

Take out Reader 6. Ask the student to read the title.

Kids Just Want to Have Fun
What do you think this book will be about? *Answers will vary*

Ask the student to read each page aloud. When the student has finished the book, ask:
  What did the children in this book like to do to have fun?
  What do you like to do to have fun?

Reader 6

Challenge

Ask students to write their own version of the story *Kids Just Want to Have Fun*. Brainstorm ideas they would like to include in their version of the book.

REVIEW F

Area	Skill	Mastery
Phonemic Awareness	Distinguish short, long, and broad vowels.	2
	Rhyme words.	3
Handwriting	Write uppercase E, O, Q, G.	2
	Write uppercase L, X, Z.	2
Phonograms	Read ar, or.	1
Reading	Read and comprehend simple sentences.	2
	Read words with broad vowels.	2
	Read words which end in double consonants.	2

Skills with a 1 should be mastered before students move on to the next lesson. For skills marked with a 2, students should demonstrate familiarity but not necessarily answer all the questions correctly. These skills will be practiced extensively in the upcoming lessons. Skills with a 3 do not need to be mastered in order for students to move on.

Phonemic Awareness Assessment

Short, Long, and Broad Vowels

F.1 Short, Long, and Broad Vowels – page 165

I will read a vowel sound. Put your finger on it. Then follow my instruction.

/ä/, broad /ä/. Circle broad /ä/.
/ī/ long /ī/. Underline long /ī/.
/ö/ broad /ö/. Put an X on broad /ö/.

Teacher Tip

Alternatively, ask the student to read each of the sounds.

Handwriting Assessment

Handwriting

F.2 Handwriting – page 166

Write one of each phonogram on your favorite line size.

Multi-Sensory Fun

If the student is not ready to write on paper, show the student the phonogram card and have him write the phonogram on a whiteboard or in a sensory box.

Phonogram Assessment

Phonogram Assessment

Ask the student to read each of the following phonogram cards: sh, th, ck, igh, ch, ee, er, wh, oi, oy, ai, ay, ng, ar, or.

Basic Phonogram Flash Cards

sh	th	ck	igh	ch	ee
er	wh	oi	oy	ai	ay
ng	ar	or			

What's That Phonogram?

F.3 What's That Phonogram? – page 167

Highlighter

On your page are groups of four phonograms. I will say a phonogram's sound(s). Color the phonogram with your highlighter.

1. /wh/
2. /ī/ three-letter /ī/
3. /är/
4. /or/
5. /ng/

Reading Assessment

Reading

F.4 What Will The Pup Do? – pages 168-169

Cut out the pictures. Read each sentence. Choose the picture that is best described.

High Frequency Words

F.5 High Frequency Words – page 171

Read each word.

Multi-Sensory Fun

Write the words on a whiteboard. Erase each one as the student reads it correctly.

Practice Ideas

Short, Long, and Broad Vowel Sounds

"Broad U" on page 154 in the Teacher's Manual
"Long, Short, and Broad Vowels" on page 163

Handwriting

Using the Tactile Cards, reteach how to write any of the phonograms which are difficult. Break down each step and have the student repeat the short, bold directions aloud.

"Optional Blind Writing" on page 40
"Phonogram Baseball" on page 54
"Phonogram Challenge" on page 75
"Sensory Writing" on page 148
"Finger Painting" on page 164

Teacher Tip

Students who struggle with handwriting should practice writing using large motor movements. It is also beneficial for these students to recite the bold, rhythmic directions aloud when writing.

Phonograms

"Go Fish" on page 67
"Timed Phonogram Reading" on page 72
"Last One!" on page 82
"Phonogram Boat Race" on page 86

"Speed Writing" on page 106
"Phonogram Slap" on page 108
"Phonogram Tight Rope" on page 159
"Phonogram Memory" on page 121

High Frequency Words

"Fox in the Hen House" on page 170

Objectives

PHONEMIC AWARENESS: Test multi-letter vowels and consonants.

PHONOGRAM: Learn `tch`.

SPELLING RULE: Three-letter /ch/ is used only after a single vowel which says its short or broad sound.

SPELLING: catch, watch, hill, glass, rope

Materials

NEEDED: LOE whiteboard, Basic Phonogram Flash Cards `tch`, `igh`, `ng`, `ay`, `ai`, `oy`, `oi`, `ee`, `sh`, `th`, bell, hat, chair, ball, glass of water, toy dog, rug, toy car, shorts, watch, fork

OPTIONAL: Phonogram Game Tiles, timer, scissors, bucket

Phonogram

The Phonogram `tch`

Show the Phonogram Card `tch`.

> This says /ch/. What does it say? */ch/*
> How many letters are in this spelling of /ch/? *three*
> We will call this three-letter /ch/.
> What is it called? *three-letter /ch/*
> Write three-letter /ch/ three times on your whiteboard.

> On your whiteboard write another phonogram that says /ch/.

Whiteboard
Basic Phonogram Flash Card `tch`

The students write ch.

> What other sounds does that form of /ch/ make? */ch-k-sh/*
> How are three-letter /ch/ and /ch-k-sh/ related? *They both say /ch/. They both have a C and an H.*

> Erase your whiteboard. I will try to confuse you. Write what I say. I will say them faster and faster.

> /ch-k-sh/

The students write ch.

three-letter /ch/
The student writes tch.

three-letter /ch/
The student writes tch.

Continue as a game.

Phonogram Practice

Phonogram Tic-Tac-Toe

71.1 Tic-Tac-Toe – pages 173-174

Two students should work together, or the teacher may work with the student. Decide who will play X's and who will play O's. Choose a phonogram and read the sound(s) aloud. If you read it correctly you may place an X or an O on the square. Proceed as if playing Tic-Tac-Toe until one player places three in a row or a tie is declared.

Challenge

Ask the students to create their own phonogram Tic-Tac-Toe game.

Phonemic Awareness

Testing Vowels

A long time ago we learned the difference between a consonant and a vowel.

What is a vowel? *A vowel is a sound you can sing and your mouth is open.*

What is a consonant? *A consonant is a sound that is blocked and it cannot be sung with the mouth open.*

Today we will test multi-letter phonograms to discover if they are consonants or vowels. *Multi* means many. So a multi-letter phonogram is a phonogram with many letters.

Show the Phonogram Card .
Is this a multi-letter phonogram? *yes*
Why? *It has more than one letter.*
Is it a vowel or a consonant? *vowel*
Why? *I can sing the sound /ī/, and my mouth is open.*

Basic Phonogram Flash Cards

tch	igh	ng	ay	ai
oy	oi	ee	sh	th

Multi-Sensory Fun

Designate a place on one side of the room to stack consonants and a place on the opposite side of the room to stack vowels. Each time a student identifies a sound correctly as a consonant or a vowel, have her run and place it in the correct pile.

Reading Practice

Reading Game

71.4 Reading Game – pages 177-180

Today you will have a set of directions to follow. Read each step and act it out using the objects that are in front of you.

Bell, hat, chair, ball, glass of water, toy dog, rug, toy car, shorts, watch, fork

Timer

Scissors

Bucket

Teacher Tip

For students who struggle with tracking, have them fold the paper like an accordion so that it is open to only one line at a time. Or use a blank sheet of paper to cover the extra lines.

Multi-Sensory Fun

Time the students. Or cut apart each direction and put it in a bucket. Draw an action to perform.

LESSON 72

Objectives

PHONEMIC AWARENESS: Strategies for reading phonograms with multiple sounds.

PHONOGRAM: Learn ow .

SPELLING: cow, snow, tell, corn, hatch

Materials

NEEDED: LOE whiteboard, Basic Phonogram Flash Card ow , Phonogram Game Cards, scissors, timer

OPTIONAL: Phonogram Game Tiles

Phonograms

The Phonogram ow

Show the Phonogram Card ow .

This says /ow-ō/. What does it say? *ow-ō*

Write /ow-ō/ three times on your whiteboard.

Whiteboard
Basic Phonogram Flash Card ow

Phonemic Awareness

Reading Phonograms with Multiple Sounds

Today we will practice words that use this phonogram.

Hold up ow .

What does this say? *ow-o*

When a word ends in /ow-ō/ we will need to try each sound and decide which one makes sense. Let's practice with a few words.

Write *how* on the board.

When trying a sound, begin with the first sound. This sound is the most common.

179

/h-ow/
Does /how/ make sense? *yes*

Let's try another.

Write *snow* on the board.

We will begin with the first sound /ow/. */s-n-ow/*
Does that makes sense? *no*
Let's try /ō/. */s-n-ō/*
Does /snō/ make sense? *yes*

Write *cow* on the board.

/k-ow/ Yes, /kow/ makes sense.

Write *mow* on the board.

/m-ow/ does not make sense. I will try /ō/. /m-ō/. Yes, /mō/ makes sense.

72.1 OW words – pages 181-182

Cut out the words in your workbook. Read each one. As you read them, sort them into two piles: words that end in /ow/ and words that end in /ō/.

Scissors

72.2 Matching – pages 183-184

Read the sentence aloud. When you see /ow-ō/, first try /ow/ and then try /ō/ to decide which one makes the most sense. Then match the sentence to the picture.

Phonogram Practice

Snatch the Phonogram

Place a pile of Phonogram Game Cards at one end of the room. Designate a starting line on the opposite side of the room. Place a whiteboard at the starting line. Read a phonogram's sound(s). The student must write it on the whiteboard, run to the other side of the room, find the phonogram in the pile, and run back. Time the student on writing and finding five to ten phonograms.

Whiteboard
Timer
Phonogram Game Cards

Spelling

Spelling List

Teach the words using the steps for Spelling Analysis. Direct students to write the words on their whiteboards or with Phonogram Game Tiles.

Word	Sentence	Say to Spell	Markings	Spelling Hints
1. cow	*The cow mooed.*	kow	c<u>ow</u>	Underline /ow/.
2. snow	*Let's play in the snow.*	snō	sn<u>ow</u>²	Underline /ō/. Put a 2 over it. /ow-ō/ said its second sound.
3. tell	*I will tell you a secret.*	tĕl	tell	We often double F, L, and S after a single vowel at the end of a base word.
4. corn	*The hen pecked at the corn.*	korn	c<u>or</u>n	Underline /or/.
5. hatch	*The eggs will hatch in two days.*	hăch	ha<u>tch</u>	Underline three-letter /ch/. Three-letter /ch/ is used only after a single vowel which says its short or broad sound.

Vocabulary Development

Opposites

I will say a word and you tell me a word that is opposite.

kind	*mean*
pretty	*ugly*
tiny	*huge, big*

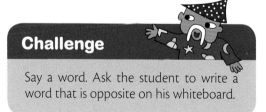

Challenge

Say a word. Ask the student to write a word that is opposite on his whiteboard.

72.3 Opposites – page 185

Read the words in the first column. Draw a line from each word to its opposite.

Reading Comprehension

Reading Comprehension

72.4 Sheep – pages 186-188

Cut out the pictures of the sheep. Lay them on the table in front of you. As you read the story aloud, line up the sheep in the order of his activities for the day.

Scissors

Teacher Tip

Some students struggle with reading so much text on one page. If the student needs help tracking, try one of the following options. 1) Use two blank pieces of paper to isolate a single line of text to read. 2) Ask the child to find the upper-case letter. Direct the child to follow the text with his finger until he reaches the end mark, but not reading the text. Then ask the child to use a highlighter to highlight the complete sentence. Finally, ask the child to read the sentence aloud. Repeat with the next sentence using a different color of highlighter.

Handwriting

Handwriting Practice

72.5 Handwriting – page 189

This handwriting sheet is optional. Ask the student to read the sentence aloud before writing it.

Challenge

Dictate the sentence aloud for the student to write on a separate sheet of paper or on her whiteboard.

LESSON 73

Objectives

PHONEMIC AWARENESS: Strategies for reading phonograms with multiple sounds.

PHONOGRAM: Learn ou .

SPELLING: out, round, what, less, sting

Materials

NEEDED: LOE whiteboard, Basic Phonogram Flash Cards ou and ow , timer, 15 Basic Phonogram Flash Cards to practice, pennies or tokens for Bingo, Lazy Vowel Chart

OPTIONAL: Phonogram Game Tiles, scissors, book from book list

Phonograms

The Phonogram ou

Show the Phonogram Card ou .
This says /ow-ō-ö-ŭ/.
How many sounds is /ow-ō-ö-ŭ/? *four*
What does it say? */ow-ō-ö-ŭ/*

Whiteboard
Basic Phonogram Flash Cards ou and ow

Show the Phonogram Card ow .
What does this say? */ow-ō/*

Show the Phonogram Cards ow and ou .
What is the same about these phonograms? *They both start with O. They both say /ow-ō/.*
What is different? *One ends in a W. One ends in a U. OU says two more sounds, /ö-ŭ/.*
Which one may I use at the end of the word? *OW*
Why can't I use OU? *English words do not end in I, U, V, or J.*
Write /ow-ō-ö-ŭ/ three times on your whiteboard.

183

Phonemic Awareness

Reading Strategies

When we have a phonogram that says many sounds, sometimes we will need to try more than one sound when reading a word.

Show the Phonogram Card ou .

What does it say? */ow-ō-ö-ŭ/*

Today I will write a word on the board. Read the word to me by sounding it out. Begin by trying the first sound, /ow/. If that does not make sense, then try the second sound, /ō/. If that does not make sense, then try the next sound.

When you know the word, shout it out.

loud	pound	
four	count	
sour	young	cloud
you	shout	your

What sound of /ow-ō-ö-ŭ/ did you hear in most of the words? */ow/*

Phonogram Practice

Phonogram Race

Set a timer for one minute. Say the sound(s) of a phonogram. The student should write it and show it to you. When he writes it correctly, say the next phonogram. See how many he can write in one minute. Then do it again and see if he can beat his first time.

Whiteboard
Timer
15 Basic Phonogram Flash Cards

Classroom: Phonogram Race

Provide each student with a whiteboard. Explain that you will time the class on how quickly they can write all fifteen phonograms correctly. Each student should write the phonogram and hold it up for you to see. If it is not written correctly, you will point at it. The student must fix it. They may help each other by looking at someone else's whiteboard or asking for

Whiteboard for each student
Timer
15 Basic Phonogram Flash Cards

someone to show them how to write it. When the whole class shows it correctly, read the next phonogram. See if the class can beat their initial time. To simplify the game, choose 3-5 phonograms to practice.

Spelling

Spelling List

Teach the words using the steps for Spelling Analysis. Direct students to write the words on their whiteboards or with Phonogram Game Tiles.

Word	Sentence	Say to Spell	Markings	Spelling Hints
1. out	The teacher went out of the room.	owt	<u>ou</u>t	Underline /ow/.
2. round	Balls are round.	rownd	r<u>ou</u>nd	Underline /ow/.
3. what	What time is it?	whät	<u>wh</u>ät	(See dialog below) Underline /wh/. Put two dots over the /ä/. /ă-ā-ä/ said its broad sound.
4. less	There is less water in this cup than in that one.	lĕs	less	We often double F, L, and S after a single vowel at the end of a base word.
5. sting	Did the bee sting you?	stĭng	sti<u>ng</u>	Underline /ng/.

what

The third word is *what*. What time is it? *what*

Lazy Vowel Chart

Did you maybe hear a schwa sound in *what*? **yes**

It <u>is</u> a schwa sound! In this case, it is the phonogram /ă-ā-ä/ being lazy and saying /ə/.

If we say the vowel clearly, it would say /wh-ä-t/. Use /ă-ā-ä/ to spell the broad sound.

Let's sound it out. */wh-ä-t/*

Now write /wh-ä-t/ on your whiteboard. Be sure to use /ă-ā-ä/.

The student writes *what* on her whiteboard

Now help me to write it by sounding it out. */wh-ä-t/*

The teacher writes *what* on the board.

Do you see any multi-letter phonograms we should underline? */wh/*

Good. Underline /wh/.

What sound is /ă-ā-ä/ saying? *its lazy sound /ə/*
What sound of /ă-ā-ä/ do we say to spell so we can remember how to spell *what*? *its broad sound, /ä/*
How do we mark the broad sound? **with two dots**
But how do we usually read this word? */whət/*
Let's add *what* to the lazy vowel chart.

Book List

Bob Books Set 2
Rub-a-Dub

Reading Practice

Matching

73.1 Matching – pages 190-191

Read the sentence. Match it to the correct picture.

Scissors

Multi-Sensory Fun

Cut out the pictures and sentences and put them at opposite ends of the room. Ask the students to choose a sentence, run over to find the picture, then place the match in a third location.

Fluency Practice

Bingo

73.2 Bingo – page 192

Direct the student to read a word on the Bingo board aloud, then cover the word. Read until the whole board is covered. If there is more than one student, direct the students to take turns reading the words.

Pennies or tokens for Bingo

Challenge

Ask the student to read the words as she uncovers each square.

Handwriting

Handwriting Practice

73.3 Handwriting – page 193

This handwriting sheet is optional. Ask the student to read the sentence aloud before writing it.

Challenge

Dictate the sentence aloud for the student to write on a separate sheet of paper or on her whiteboard.

Objectives

PHONEMIC AWARENESS: Strategies for reading phonograms with multiple sounds.

PHONOGRAM: Learn ough.

SPELLING: was, thought, that, wall, king

Materials

NEEDED: LOE whiteboard, Basic Phonogram Flash Card ough, blocks or LEGO®s, Lazy Vowel Chart, playdough, alphabet cookie cutters, stick, scissors

OPTIONAL: Phonogram Game Tiles, books from book list

Phonograms

The Phonogram ough

Show the Phonogram Card ough.

This says /ŏ-ō-ö-ow-ŭf-ŏf/.

I will say that again. This time count the sounds. /ŏ-ō-ö-ow-ŭf-ŏf/

How many sounds is that? *six*

Let's say it together. */ŏ-ō-ö-ow-ŭf-ŏf/*

Let's march around the room saying the sounds. */ŏ-ō-ö-ow-ŭf-ŏf/*

Write /ŏ-ō-ö-ow-ŭf-ŏf/ three times on your whiteboard.

The student writes *ough.*

Which one is the neatest?

Put a smiley face next to it.

Whiteboard

Basic Phonogram Flash Card ough

Teacher Tip

OUGH has the most sounds of any phonogram. In addition, it is only found in twenty-two base words. Nevertheless, several of these words are high frequency words that need to be mastered by young readers. For a complete list of OUGH words see the *Phonogram and Spelling Rule Quick Reference.*

Phonemic Awareness

Phonograms with Multiple Sounds

74.1 OUGH Words – page 194

OUGH has six sounds. This can be a little challenging for reading.

Read the sentence aloud. When you get to the OUGH word, try each of the sounds until you find one that makes sense. When you have finished the sentence, go back and read the whole sentence to me again.

Each time you read an OUGH word correctly, add a block to the tower. When you have reached the end of the page, you may knock it down.

Blocks or LEGO®s

Challenge

Ask the student to read the sentence quietly in his head. When he has figured out the whole sentence, have him read it aloud.

Phonogram Practice

Phonogram Playdough

Write the word *playdough* on the board.

Today we will practice our phonograms using this.

Point to the word *playdough*.

What does this say? /p-l-ā d-ō/ *playdough*

Playdough
Alphabet cookie cutters
Stick

Encourage students to cut letters out of playdough and to read the sounds. Also ask them to form multi-letter phonograms and words with the playdough. The students may also roll out the dough and use a stick to write the phonograms in the dough.

Spelling

Spelling List

Teach the words using the steps for Spelling Analysis. Direct students to write the words on their whiteboards or with Phonogram Game Tiles.

Word	Sentence	Say to Spell	Markings	Spelling Hints
1. was	*She was on my team.*	wăz	wäs²	Put two dots over the /ä/. /ă-ā-ä/ said its broad sound. Tip: A often says its broad sound after a W. Put a 2 over the /z/. /s-z/ said its second sound.
2. thought	*I thought it was later.*	thŏt	<u>th</u>ou<u>gh</u>t	Underline /th/. Underline /ŏ/.
3. that	*That is a great idea!*	THăt	<u>th</u>at²	Underline /TH/. Put a 2 over /th-TH/. It said its second sound /TH/.
4. wall	*Bounce the ball against the wall.*	wäl	wäll	Put two dots over the /ä/. /ă-ā-ä/ said its broad sound. We often double F, L, and S after a single vowel at the end of a base word.
5. king	*The king is wearing a crown.*	kĭng	kĭ<u>ng</u>	Underline /ng/.

was

The first word is *was*. She was on my team. *was*

Did you hear a schwa sound in *was*? **yes**

The phonogram /ă-ā-ä/ is being lazy and saying /ə/.

If we say the vowel clearly, it would say, /w-ä-z/. Use /ă-ā-ä/ to spell the broad sound.

Let's sound it out. **/w-ä-z/**

Now write /w-ä-z/ on your whiteboard. Be sure to use /ă-ā-ä/. Use /s-z/ for the last sound.

The student writes *was* on her whiteboard.

Now help me to write it by sounding it out. **/w-ä-z/**

The teacher writes *was* on the board.

What sound is /ă-ā-ä/ saying? **its lazy sound /ə/**

What sound of /ă-ā-ä/ do we say to spell so we can remember how to spell *was*? **its broad sound, /ä/**

How do we mark the broad sound? **with two dots**

Lazy Vowel Chart

How should we mark /z/? *write a 2 over it because it is the second sound of /s-z/*

How do we usually read this word? */wəz/*

Let's add *was* to the lazy vowel chart.

Reading Comprehension

Riddles

74.2 What Am I? – pages 195-196

Cut along the dotted lines. Fold the paper in half. Read the riddle on the front. Guess what is being described. Open the flap and circle the answer.

I am round. You hit me with sticks or pound on me with your hands. I am loud. What am I? drum

I make a sound. I wake him up. I have a bell. I tick. What am I? clock

I grow on a tree. I am sour. I am green. What am I? lime

Scissors

Teacher Tip

If the student does not know the answer, have him brainstorm possibilities. For students who need to build confidence, write some options on the board and have the students choose the correct answer.

Handwriting

Handwriting Practice

74.3 Handwriting – page 197

This handwriting sheet is optional. Ask the student to read the sentence aloud before writing it.

Challenge

Dictate the sentence aloud for the student to write on a separate sheet of paper or on her whiteboard.

Book List

Bob Books Set 2
   The Big Hat
   Bow-wow
   Fun in the Sun

Objectives

PHONEMIC AWARENESS: Review syllables and plurals.

SPELLING: I, you, your, flour, dough

READER 7

Materials

NEEDED: LOE whiteboard, two sets of Phonogram Game Cards, timer, cloth bag, Reader 7

OPTIONAL: Phonogram Game Tiles

Phonemic Awareness

Syllables

What is a syllable? *A syllable is the beat in words.*

What are two ways we can count how many syllables are in a word? *Put my hand under my chin and feel how many times my mouth opens to say the vowel sound, or hum the word.*

How many syllables in *turtle*? */hm-hm/ two syllables*

How many syllables in *popcorn*? */hm-hm/ two syllables*

How many syllables in *bicycle*? */hm-hm-hm/ three syllables*

75.1 Syllables – page 198

Look at the pictures on the page. Say the name of the object. Then hum the word. Circle the number of syllables in the word.

Plurals

75.2 Plurals – page 199

A while ago we talked about how to make a word plural. Do you remember what plural means? *answers will vary*

I will write a few words on the board. See if you can remember what plural means.

As you write the first word, say "This is NOT plural."
As you write the second word, say "This is plural."

ball	balls
cow	cows
chair	chairs
cake	cakes
egg	eggs

Plural means more than one.

What do we add to a word to make it plural? */s-z/*
On your worksheet you have pictures. Fill in the blanks to make the words plural.

Phonogram Practice

Rotten Egg

Place all the Phonogram Game Cards in the bag with the Rotten Egg card(s). Set the timer for an undisclosed time of 1-3 minutes. Players take turns drawing a card and reading the phonogram aloud. If a player reads the phonogram correctly, he keeps the card and passes the bag to the next player. If he does not read the phonogram correctly, he must put the card back into the bag and pass the bag to the next person. If a student draws the Rotten Egg card, he must put all his cards back into the bag and pass it to the next player. Play ends when the timer beeps. The student holding the most cards wins.

2 sets of Phonogram Game Cards
1-2 Rotten Egg cards
Timer
Cloth bag

Spelling

Spelling List

Teach the words using the steps for Spelling Analysis. Direct students to write the words on their whiteboards or with Phonogram Game Tiles.

	Word	Sentence	Say to Spell	Markings	Spelling Hints
1.	I	*I am cold.*	ī	ī	Put a line over the /ī/. It said its long sound. Notice we always write this word with an uppercase I.
2.	you	*You are my friend.*	yö	y<u>ou</u>³	Underline /ö/. Put a 3 over it. /ow-ō-ö-ŭ/ said its third sound /ö/.
3.	your	*Your house is next to mine.*	yōr	y<u>ou</u>²r	Underline /ō/. Put a 2 over it. /ow-ō-ö-ŭ/ said its second sound. Note that you and your are related in meaning. This is an example of how English spelling works to represent both sound and meaning.
4.	flour	*The flour spilled on the floor.*	flowr	fl<u>ou</u>r	Underline the /ow/.
5.	dough	*The bread dough is rising.*	dō	d<u>ough</u>²	Underline /ō/. Put a 2 over it. /ŏ-ō-ö-ow-uf-ŏf/ said its second sound.

I

The first word is *I.* I am cold. *I*
Sound it out. */ī/*
Use /ĭ-ī-ē-y/.
When we write the word *I*, we do something special. We always use an uppercase letter.
How will your write I? **with an uppercase letter**
Now write /ī/ on your whiteboard. Be sure to use an uppercase /ĭ-ī-ē-y/.
The student writes *I* on her whiteboard.

Now help me to write it by sounding it out. */ī/*
The teacher writes *I* on the board.

Teacher Tip

I, you, and *thou* are English words that do end in I and U. These are true and rare exceptions to the rule that English words do not end in I, U, V, or J. To learn more, see *Uncovering the Logic of English* pp. 51-56.

Let's read it together. /ī/

Do you notice anything that is strange about this word? *answers will vary*

Does it break any of our rules? *English words do not end in I, U, V, or J.*

Hmm. That is strange. We will talk about it in a minute.

you

The second word is *you*. You are my friend. *you*

Sound it out. /y-ö/

Use /ow-ō-ö-ŭ/.

Now write /y-ö/ on your whiteboard.

The student writes *you* on her whiteboard.

Now help me to write it by sounding it out. /y-ö/

The teacher writes *you* on the board.

Let's read it together. /y-ö/

How will we mark it? *Underline the /ö/ and put a three over it. /ow-ō-ö-ŭ/ said its third sound /ö/.*

Do you notice anything that is strange about this word?
Answers will vary

Does it break any of our rules? *English words do not end in I, U, V, or J.*

Now we have two words in our spelling list that break the rule. What are the words? *you and I*

Do you know why *you* and *I* can break the rule? You and I can break this rule because you and I are very special.

Do most of the words follow the rule that English words do not end in I, U, V, or J? *yes*

Teacher Tip

If the student forgets how to write /ow-ō-ö-ŭ/, simply show him the phonogram card or write it on the board.

Reading

Reader

Reader 7

Take out Reader 7. Ask the student to read the title.

Time to Bake

What do you think this book will be about?

Ask the student to read each page aloud. When he has finished the book, ask:

Something funny happened in this story. What was it? *There was a chick in the egg.*

Handwriting

Handwriting Practice

75.3 Handwriting – page 200

This handwriting sheet is optional. Ask the student to read the sentence aloud before writing it.

Challenge

Dictate the sentence aloud for the student to write on a separate sheet of paper or on her whiteboard.

REVIEW G

Area	Skill	Mastery
Phonemic Awareness	Add an -S to make a word plural.	1
Handwriting	Write uppercase L, X, Z.	2
	Copy a sentence with an uppercase letter and punctuation.	2
Phonograms	Read tch, ow, ou, ough.	2
Reading	Read and comprehend simple sentences.	2
	Read words which include phonograms that have multiple sounds.	2
	Read words which end in double consonants.	1

Skills with a 1 should be mastered before students move on to the next lesson. For skills marked with a 2, students should demonstrate familiarity but not necessarily answer all the questions correctly. These skills will be practiced extensively in the upcoming lessons.

Phonemic Awareness Assessment

Plurals

G.1 Plurals – page 201

Look at the picture. Add an -S if it is needed to make the word plural.

Handwriting Assessment

Handwriting

G.2 Handwriting – page 202

Choose your favorite line size. Read the sentence, then write it.

Phonogram Assessment

Phonogram Assessment

Ask the student to read each of the following phonogram cards: tch, ow, ou, ough.

Basic Phonogram Flash Cards

| tch | ow | ou | ough |

What's That Phonogram?

G.3 What's That Phonogram? – page 203

Highlighter

On your page are groups of four phonograms. I will say a phonogram's sound(s). Color the phonogram with your highlighter.

1. /ch/ three-letter /ch/
2. /ŏ-ō-ö-ow-ŭf-öf/
3. /ow-ō-ö-ŭ/
4. /ow-ō/

Reading Assessment

Reading

G.4 Matching – pages 204-205

Read the sentence. Match it to the correct picture.

High Frequency Words

G.5 High Frequency Words – page206

Read each word.

Teacher Tip

Ask students to read the sentences aloud. Observe the strategies the student uses to decode the words which have multiple options for sounds.

Multi-Sensory Fun

Write the words on index cards and hide them around the room.

Practice Ideas

Handwriting

Using the Tactile Cards, reteach how to write any of the phonograms which are difficult. Break down each step and have the student repeat the short, bold directions aloud.

"Optional Blind Writing" on page 40
"Phonogram Baseball" on page 54
"Phonogram Challenge" on page 75
"Sensory Writing" on page 148
"Finger Painting" on page 164
"Phonogram Race" on page 184

Teacher Tip

Students who struggle with handwriting should practice writing using large motor movements. It is also beneficial for these students to recite the bold, rhythmic directions aloud when writing.

Phonograms

High Frequency Words

Reading

LESSON 76

Objectives

PHONEMIC AWARENESS: Practice rhyming words.

SPELLING: pay, paid, say, said, white

Materials

NEEDED: LOE whiteboard, Basic Phonogram Flash Cards, red and black dry-erase markers, scissors

OPTIONAL: Phonogram Game Tiles, large whiteboard, small soft ball, NERF® gun with suction cup darts, index cards

Phonemic Awareness

Rhyming

Ask the child to stand on one end of the room.

> Today we will play a rhyming game. I will say a word. You then need to say a word that rhymes with it. For each rhyming word, you may take one step forward. When you cannot think of any more words that rhyme, I will give you a new word.

log	*hog, dog, frog, cog, bog, clog*
call	*fall, wall, mall, stall, hall, small*
nose	*hose, rose, toes, chose, those, close*
now	*how, cow, plow, sow, wow*
snake	*lake, make, rake, bake, flake, shake, take*
hat	*bat, cat, mat, sat, fat, at, gnat, flat, pat, rat*
may	*tray, bay, say, lay, day, hay, they, ray, way*

76.1 Rhymes – page 207

Read the words. Draw a line to match the words that rhyme.

Teacher Tip

If the student struggles with rhyming, isolate the ending sound of the word and ask the student to think of words that end in ___.

Large whiteboard
Small, soft ball
NERF gun with suction cup darts

Multi-Sensory Fun

Write the words on a whiteboard. Ask the student to read the words and toss a ball at the words that rhyme or shoot them with a NERF® gun.

Phonogram Practice

Phonogram Practice

Show the cards and ask the students to read the sounds and jump as they read each sound.

Basic Phonogram Flash Cards

Spelling

Spelling List

Teach the words using the steps for Spelling Analysis. Direct students to write the words on their whiteboards or with Phonogram Game Tiles.

Refer to the suggested scripting on the next page before teaching these words.

Teacher Tip

In this lesson, there is only one challenge word. Be sure to teach all of the first four words to the students. *Said* is not a challenge word. It is a necessary part of the lesson.

	Word	Sentence	Say to Spell	Markings	Spelling Hints
1.	pay	*How much did you pay for that game?*	pā	p<u>ay</u>	Underline two letter /ā/. English words do not end in I, U, V, or J. Therefore we must use AY.
2.	paid	*I paid twenty dollars.*	pād	p<u>ai</u>d	Underline two-letter /ā/.
3.	say	*Did she say what time we are leaving?*	sā	s<u>ay</u>	Underline two letter /ā/. English words do not end in I, U, V, or J. Therefore we must use AY.
4.	said	*She said we will go at five o'clock.*	sād	s<u>ai</u>d	Underline two letter /ā/. See the notes for teaching this word.
5.	white	*He wore a white shirt to work.*	whīt	<u>wh</u>īt<u>e</u>	Underline /wh/. Put a line over the /ī/. Double underline the silent final E. The vowel said its long sound because of the E.

pay

The first word is *pay*. How much did you pay for that game? *pay*

Let's sound out *pay*. /p-ā/

What kind of /ā/ will you use? **Two-letter ā that you may use at the end of English words.**

Write *pay* on your whiteboard. Sound it out as you write it. /p-ā/

Now help me to write it. /p-ā/

How will we mark *pay*? **Underline the two-letter /ā/.**

paid

The second word is *paid*. I paid twenty dollars. *paid*

Let's sound out *paid*. /p-ā-d/

What kind of /ā/ will you use? **Two-letter ā that you may not use at the end of English words.**

Write *paid* on your whiteboard. Sound it out as you write it. /p-ā-d/

Now help me to write it. /p-ā-d/

How will we mark *paid*? **Underline the two-letter /ā/.**

How are *pay* and *paid* related? **They both mean to pay for something. They use the two-letter /ā/ phonograms AI and AY.**

say

The third word is *say*. Did she say what time we are leaving? *say*

Let's sound out *say*. /s-ā/

What kind of /ā/ will you use? **Two-letter ā that you may use at the end of English words.**

Write *say* on your whiteboard. Sound it out as you write it. /s-ā/

Now help me to write it. /s-ā/

How will we mark *say*? **Underline the two-letter /ā/.**

said

The fourth word is *said*. She said we will go at 5 o'clock. *said*

This word has a problem. I will write *said* and I want you to tell me what the problem is.

Write *said* on the board.

It has a two-letter /ā/ in it but we say /ĕ/.

Let's sound out *said*. /s-ā-d/

But how do we usually say the word? /sĕd/

Maybe at one time people would have pronounced this /sād/. But the pronunciation changed over time.

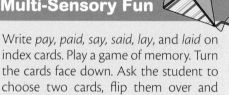

Index cards

Multi-Sensory Fun

Write *pay, paid, say, said, lay,* and *laid* on index cards. Play a game of memory. Turn the cards face down. Ask the student to choose two cards, flip them over and read them. If they are related in meaning, he may keep the match. If they are not related in meaning he should turn them back upside down and go again.

Teacher Tip

Say and *said* are following a pattern for irregular verbs like *lay* and *pay*. It is likely that *said* was at one time pronounced with a long /ā/ sound. Words with exceptions to the phonics rules may often be explained through morphology. It is helpful for many students to know that there is a reason for the spelling, the language is not simply riddled with random spellings.

Write *said* on your whiteboard. Sound it out as you write it. */s-ā-d/*

Now help me to write it. */s-ā-d/*

How will we mark *said*? *Underline the two-letter /ā/*

How are *say* and *said* related? *They both mean to speak. They use the two-letter /ā/ phonograms AI and AY.*

Handwriting

Handwriting Practice

76.2 Handwriting – page 208

This handwriting sheet is optional. Ask the student to read the sentence aloud before writing it.

Challenge

Dictate the sentence aloud for the student to write on a separate sheet of paper or on her whiteboard.

Reading

Reading Quotes

When someone is speaking, we have a special way to mark that in writing. I will write a sentence on the board. I want you to read it aloud and then tell me what you notice.

Red and black dry-erase markers

Write the comma and the quotation marks in red. Write: Dad said, "It is time to go."

Point to the quotation marks.

These are called quotation marks. Whatever is between them is what is being said by the person.

I will read the quote. When I read what is in the quotes, I can even change my voice to sound like the person.

Read the quote with a dramatic flair by changing your voice to sound like "Dad."

I will write a second quote on the board. Let's read it together.

Write: Pam said, "I found a coin."

Read it again and this time try to sound like Pam.

76.3 Reading Quotes – pages 209-210

Cut out each of the sentences. Fold them in half. Then we will play a game. Choose a quote. Read it quietly to yourself. Think of who is speaking and what kind of voice the person would have. Then read the quote aloud using a voice that sounds like the person speaking.

Scissors

Objectives

PHONEMIC AWARENESS: Learn the reasons for the spellings of say, said, and says.

SPELLING: says, down, right, deer, make

Materials

NEEDED: LOE whiteboard, scissors, Basic Phonogram Flash Cards, buzzer, word bucket

OPTIONAL: Phonogram Game Tiles, toy car

Phonemic Awareness

Say, Said, Says

Write *pay*, *paid*, and *pays* on the board.

What do these say? *pay, paid, pays*

Use them in a sentence. *Answers will vary.*

How are these words related? *They all mean the same thing. They use two-letter /ā/ that you may use at the end of English words or two-letter /ā/ that you may not use at the end of English words.*

Write *lay*, *laid*, and *lays* on the board.

Read these words. *lay, laid, lays*

Use them in a sentence. *Answers will vary.*

How are these words related? *They all mean the same thing. They use two-letter /ā/ that you may use at the end of English words or two-letter /ā/ that you may not use at the end of English words.*

Write *say* and *said* on the board.

Read these words. *say, said*

Use each one in a sentence. *Answers will vary.*

What do you notice? *They are related in meaning. They use two-letter /ā/ that you may use at the end of English words or two-letter /ā/ that you may not use at the end of English words.*

This is not the only word where two-letter /ā/ says /ĕ/.

Write *says* on the board.

What do you think this says?

I will read it for you. /s-ĕ-z/ /sĕz/

Use *says* in a sentence. **Answers will vary.**

How is *says* related to *say* and *said*? **It means the same thing. It uses a two-letter /ā/. Like in said, two-letter /ā/ is saying /ĕ/.**

Maybe people at one time pronounced this words /sāz/.

77.1 Find It! – pages 211-212

Cut out the words. Hide them throughout the room.

Scissors

I hid nine words in the room. Find all nine words, bring them to me, and read them.

We can think of these words as being part of different groups.

Which words do you think are related in spelling? For example, *pay* and *lay* both end in two-letter AY that we may use at the end of English words. How can you group the words to show they have related spellings?

pay, lay, say
pays, lays, says
paid, laid, said

Now let's group the words a different way. How can we group the words to show they are related in meaning? For example, *pay* and *paid* have a related meaning.

pay, paid, pays
lay, laid, lays
say, said, says

Teacher Tip

This exercise demonstrates to the students an explanation for the words *says* and *said*. This provides a memory hook to aid students in mastering these words. Notice that even with words that do not follow the phonics rules, we are still able to draw a logical connection to morphology. If we spelled these words exactly how they sound, we would lose the visual relationship in meaning.

Phonogram Practice

Teacher Trouble

Provide the student with a stack of Phonogram Cards. The student needs to quiz the teacher by reading a phonogram for the teacher to write. The teacher should make several "mistakes." When the teacher makes a mistake, the student may ring a buzzer.

Basic Phonogram Flash Cards
Whiteboard
Buzzer

Spelling

Spelling List

Teach the words using the steps for Spelling Analysis. Direct students to write the words on their whiteboards or with Phonogram Game Tiles.

Word	Sentence	Say to Spell	Markings	Spelling Hints
1. says	*She says it is five miles to the end of the path.*	sāz	sa̲y̲s	Say to spell /sāz/. Underline two-letter /ā/. Put a 2 over the /z/. /s-z/ said its second sound.
2. down	*She slid down the slide.*	down	do̲w̲n	Underline /ow/.
3. right	*Turn right at the corner.*	rīt	ri̲g̲h̲t	Underline three-letter /ī/.
4. deer	*The deer ran across the road.*	dēr	de̲e̲r	Underline E double E, which always says /ē/.
5. make	*We will make dinner in one hour.*	māk	māke̲	Draw a line over the /ā/. It said its long sound. Double underline the silent final E. The vowel said its long sound because of the E.

Teacher Tip

Discuss the relationship between say - says, pay - pays, lay - lays. Recall how *says* may have been pronounced with a long /a/ at one time. This is a true exception to the phonograms and rules, but the spelling is shaped by the word's meaning.

Reading Comrehension

Who Said What?

77.2 Who Said What? – pages 213-214

Read the quote. Look at the pictures. Decide who said it and draw a line to match the quote to the person.

Fluency

Reading Maze

77.3 High Frequency Words – pages 215-216

Cut out the new words and add them to the Word Bucket. Remove the action cards, leaving only the word cards in the bucket.

> Today we will build a long word maze with the words you know how to read from the bucket. You need to pull out a word and read it. If you read it without my help, we will put it in this line. If you need help, we will put it in a pile to practice tomorrow.

Scissors

Word Bucket from Lesson 70

Space to line words up across the floor in a maze

Toy car

Multi-Sensory Fun

Have the student zoom a car across the table for each word that is read correctly.

Teacher Tip

Allow students to sound out the words if they are unsure. Brain research shows that strong readers are sounding out words so quickly it appears to be "instantaneous." To reach this level of fluency, students will need regular practice.

Handwriting

Handwriting Practice

77.4 Handwriting – page 217

This handwriting sheet is optional. Ask the student to read the sentence aloud before writing it.

Challenge

Dictate the sentence aloud for the student to write on a separate sheet of paper or on her whiteboard.

Objectives

PHONEMIC AWARENESS: English words do not end in I, U, V, or J.

SPELLING RULE: Y says /ī/ at the end of a one-syllable word.

SPELLING: by, show, fly, pass, ate

Materials

NEEDED: LOE whiteboard, Basic Phonogram Flash Card y , large whiteboard, small soft ball

OPTIONAL: Phonogram Game Tiles, scissors, NERF® gun with suction cup darts

Spelling Rule

Y Says Long /ī/

Today you need to be a spelling detective.

Basic Phonogram Flash Card y

Show the Basic Phonogram Flash Card y .

What does this phonogram say? */y-ĭ-ī-ē/*
Today we will learn when this phonogram says the long /ī/ sound.

78.1 Spelling Mystery – page 218

In your workbook you have a list of words. I will read the beginning of the list. When you think you can continue reading the list, raise your hand and you can take over.

by	spy	fry
sky	my	shy
try	dry	why
fly		

What do you notice about the Y? *It is saying /ī/.*
When does it say /ī/? *at the end of the word*

Let's count the syllables in these words. How could you count the syllables? *Put my hand under my chin and count how many times my mouth opens.*

by   one syllable
sky   one syllable…

Y says /ī/ at the end of a one-syllable word.
Let's read the list again.

Phonemic Awareness

English Words Do Not End in I, U, V, or J

Write *tri*, *fli*, and *si* on the board.

Why can I not spell these words with an I at the end?   *English words do not end in I, U, V, or J.*

When you hear /ī/ at the end of the word, how could we spell it?   *with a /y-ĭ-ī-ē/ or with three-letter /ī/*

Read each word after I correct it.

Cross out *tri* and write *try*.
/t-r-ī/   try

Cross out *fli* and write *fly*.
/f-l-ī/   fly

Cross out *si* and write *sigh*.
/s-ī/   sigh

Hmm. Notice the words fly and sigh. Do these words rhyme?   *yes*
Why do they rhyme?   *They sound the same at the end.*
But do they look the same?   *no*
Words do not need to look the same to rhyme. They only need to end in the same sound.

Rhymes

78.2 Rhymes – page 219

Read the words. Draw a line to match the words that rhyme.

Scissors

Multi-Sensory Fun

Cut out the words. Place them in two piles on opposite sides of the room. Ask the student to choose a word, read it, run to the other side of the room, then find a word that rhymes.

Phonogram Practice

Phonogram Target

Read 5-10 phonograms' sound(s). Direct the student to write them someplace on the large whiteboard to create a target. When all the phonograms have been written, tell the student to step back 3-5 steps. Provide the student with a small, soft ball or a NERF® gun. Explain that you will now read a phonogram, and he should hit the phonogram by throwing the ball at it, or shoot it with the NERF® gun.

Large whiteboard
Small, soft ball
NERF® gun with suction cup darts

Spelling

Spelling List

Teach the words using the steps for Spelling Analysis. Direct students to write the words on their whiteboards or with Phonogram Game Tiles.

	Word	Sentence	Say to Spell	Markings	Spelling Hints
1.	by	*He lives by the lake.*	bī	by	Y said long /ī/ at the end of a one-syllable word.
2.	show	*Will you show me your drawing?*	shō	sh<u>ow</u> ²	Underline /sh/. Underline /ō/ and put a 2 over it. /ow-ō/ said its second sound /ō/.
3.	fly	*The plane will fly overhead.*	flī	fly	Y said long /ī/ at the end of a one-syllable word.
4.	pass	*Please pass the milk.*	păs	pass	We often double F, L, and S after a single vowel at the end of a base word.
5.	ate	*The dog quickly ate the scraps.*	āt	āt<u>e</u>	Put a line over the /ā/. Double underline the silent final E. The vowel said its long sound because of the E.

Reading Practice

Reading Game

78.3 Reading Basketball Game – pages 220-221

Read the story about the game. Draw a line from player to player showing how the ball traveled during the game.

Handwriting

Handwriting Practice

78.4 Handwriting – page 222

This handwriting sheet is optional. Ask the student to read the sentence aloud before writing it.

Challenge

Dictate the sentence aloud for the student to write on a separate sheet of paper or on her whiteboard.

Objectives

PHONEMIC AWARENESS: Strategies for reading phonograms with multiple sounds.

PHONOGRAM: Learn ea .

SPELLING: great, my, team, cry, grass

Materials

NEEDED: LOE whiteboard, Basic Phonogram Flash Card ea , two sets of Phonogram Game Cards, a list of High Frequency Words from Lessons 42, 48, 51, 63, 66-70, 77

OPTIONAL: Phonogram Game Tiles, scissors

Phonograms

The Phonogram ea

Show the Phonogram Card ea .

Whiteboard
Basic Phonogram Flash Card ea

This says /ē-ĕ-ā/. How many sounds is that? *three*
Let's say them together. */ē-ĕ-ā/*
Write /ē-ĕ-ā/ three times on your whiteboard.

Phonemic Awareness

The Sounds of ea

Show the Phonogram Card ea .

Basic Phonogram Flash Card ea

How many sounds does today's phonogram make? *three*
What are they? */ē-ĕ-ā/*
How will we know which sound it is saying? *answers vary*

There is not a rule that will tell us, so we will simply need to try the sound. But the first sound /ē/ is the most common. EA says /ā/ in only nine words. So when you are trying to read words with an EA, start with the first sound and see if it makes sense. If not, then try the second sound /ĕ/. If it still does not make sense, try /ā/.

79.1 The Phonogram EA – page 223

In your workbook you have five sentences. The word using the EA phonogram is in bold. Read each sentence aloud.

Take your seat.
He hit his head.
We had a great day.
Did you clean the sink?
The cow eats grass.

Teacher Tip

Some students will need to sound out the EA words and try each option. Others will be able to read it fluently from context. Both ways are acceptable at this level. Do not make a student who reads it fluently go back and try each sound. Likewise do not ask a child who is sounding it out to guess from context.

Rhymes

79.2 Rhymes – page 224

Read the words. Draw a line to match the words that rhyme.

Scissors

Multi-Sensory Fun

Cut out the words. Place them in two piles on opposite sides of the room. Ask the student to choose a word, read it, then run to the other side of the room and find a word that rhymes.

Phonogram Practice

Go Fish

Deal five cards per player. Place the remaining cards in the middle of the table face down and spread them out into a "fishing pond." The first player chooses another player to ask, "Do you have a __?" Students should ask for a phonogram that matches one in their hand by saying the sound(s). If the answer is "yes," the asking player receives the card and lays down the matched pair. The asking player then repeats his turn. If the answer is "no," the player who was asked should say, "Go fish." The asking player then draws a card from the pond. If a match is found, it is laid down and the asking player repeats his turn. If no match is found, play moves to the next player on the left. Continue to play until all the cards have been matched. The player with the most matches wins.

2 sets of Phonogram Game Cards
Choose 20-30 matching phonogram pairs.

Spelling

Spelling List

Teach the words using the steps for Spelling Analysis. Direct students to write the words on their whiteboards or with Phonogram Game Tiles.

Word	Sentence	Say to Spell	Markings	Spelling Hints
1. great	What a great color!	grāt	gr<u>ea</u>t (3 over ea)	Underline /ā/. Put a 3 over it. /ē-ĕ-ā/ said its third sound.
2. my	That is my cat.	mī	my	Y said long /ī/ at the end of a one-syllable word.
3. team	Our team won the game.	tēm	t<u>ea</u>m	Underline /ē/.
4. cry	Do not cry.	krī	cry	Y said long /ī/ at the end of a one-syllable word.
5. grass	The kittens played in the grass.	grăs	grass	We often double F, L, and S after a single vowel at the end of a base word.

Teacher Tip

Remember to finger spell while the student segments each word, and to provide a verbal hint whenever clarification is needed about which spelling to use for a sound (such as the /ē/ in *team*: "Use /ē-ĕ-ā/"). Provide all the information students need to write each word correctly.

Word Game

Eraser Race

Make a list of high frequency words that need additional practice from Lessons 42, 48, 51, 63, 66-70, and 77. Choose words the student is not reading fluently.

Whiteboard
List of High Frequency Words

Today we will have an eraser race. I will write three words on the board. You need to read the words. While you read, I will be writing new words. When you read a word correctly, I will stop writing and erase the word. See if you can catch me by reading the words faster than I can erase them.

Handwriting

Handwriting Practice

79.3 Handwriting – page 225

This handwriting sheet is optional. Ask the student to read the sentence aloud before writing it.

Challenge

Dictate the sentence aloud for the student to write on a separate sheet of paper or on her whiteboard.

Objectives

PHONEMIC AWARENESS: Change the intital sound to form new words.

PHONOGRAM: Learn $\boxed{\text{oa}}$.

SPELLING: read, won, boat, coat, head

READER 8

Materials

NEEDFD: LOE whiteboard, Basic Phonogram Flash Cards learned so far and $\boxed{\text{oa}}$, Phonogram Game Tiles, 3 bases and a home plate, Lazy Vowel Chart, scissors, Reader 8

Phonograms

The Phonogram $\boxed{\text{oa}}$

Show the Phonogram Card $\boxed{\text{oa}}$.

Whiteboard

Basic Phonogram Flash Card $\boxed{\text{oa}}$

This says /ō/. What does it say? */ō/*

This is two-letter /ō/ that we may NOT use at the end of English words.

Where can't we use this two-letter /ō/? *at the end of the word*

Where may we use it? *in the middle of the word or at the beginning of the word*

Write two-letter /ō/ that we may not use at the end of English words three times on your whiteboard.

Phonemic Awareness

Making New Words

Today we will make new words using phonogram tiles. I have arranged the letters in a pattern. I want you to read the word I have created.

Phonogram Game Tiles

c	oa	t

What does this say? *coat*

What happens if I change the /t/ to /ch/?

c	oa	ch

What does this say? *coach*

What happens if I change the /ch/ to /st/?

c	oa	s	t

What does this say? *coast*

What does it say when I change the letters like this? *soap*

s	oa	p

What happens if I change the /p/ to /k/?

s	oa	k

What does this say? *soak*

80.1 Making New Words – page 226

On your worksheet you have a matrix with starting sounds, two-letter /ō/, and final sounds. What words can you make using these phonograms?

Write them on the board as students identify them.

coat	croak	goal
coast	float	soak
coal	goat	soap

Challenge

Ask students to write the words they find on their whiteboards.

Phonogram Practice

Phonogram Baseball

Choose the location for home plate and each of the three bases. The student "up to bat" stands on home plate with a whiteboard and dry-erase marker. The teacher (or another student) chooses a phonogram card and reads it to the batter. The batter writes the phonogram on his whiteboard. If it is spelled correctly, he advances to the next base. If it is not spelled correctly, he is "out." At each base, he is given another phonogram to spell. Each time he crosses home plate, he is awarded 1 point. Three outs and the game is over.

Basic Phonogram Flash Cards

Whiteboard

3 bases and a home plate

Phonogram Baseball for the Classroom

Choose the location for home plate and each of the three bases. Divide the class into two teams. The student "up to bat" stands on home plate with a whiteboard and dry-erase marker. The teacher (or another student) chooses a phonogram card and reads it to the batter. The batter writes the phonogram on his whiteboard. If it is spelled correctly, he advances to the next base. If it is not spelled correctly, he is "out." The next "batter" then moves into position with his whiteboard. The teacher (or another student) reads a new phonogram. The batter must write it on his whiteboard correctly to advance. Likewise, each player on base must write it correctly to advance. Anyone who misspells the phonogram is "out." Each time a player crosses home plate, his team is awarded 1 point. Three outs and the team is out, and play advances to the next team.

Optional: Assign "basemen" to check the spelling at each base.

Basic Phonogram Flash Cards

4 whiteboards

3 bases and a home plate

Spelling

Spelling List

Teach the words using the steps for Spelling Analysis. Direct students to write the words on their whiteboards or with Phonogram Game Tiles.

Lazy Vowel Chart

	Word	Sentence	Say to Spell	Markings	Spelling Hints
1	read	*We will read a new book today.*	rēd	re̲a̲d	Underline /ē/. May also be said with a short /ĕ/ sound and marked with a 2 over the /ē-ĕ-ā/. For example, I read the book yesterday.
2.	won	*We won the game!*	wŏn	won	Say to spell /w-ŏ-n/. Add this word to the list of schwa words.
3.	boat	*Would you like to ride in the boat?*	bōt	bo̲a̲t	Underline two-letter /ō/.
4.	coat	*Wear your warm coat today.*	kōt	co̲a̲t	Underline two-letter /ō/.
5.	head	*He bumped his head.*	hĕd	he̲a̲d²	Underline /ĕ/. Put a 2 over it. /ē-ĕ-ā/ said its second sound /ĕ/.

won

The second word is *won*. We won the game. *won*

Place your hand under your chin and say, "won." How many syllables in *won*? **won, one**

Do you hear a sound that may be a lazy vowel sound? **yes**

We will exaggerate the vowel to say /wŏn/.

Let's sound it out. */w-ŏ-n/*

Use an /ŏ-ō-ö/.

The student writes *won* on his whiteboard.

It is now my turn to write *won*. Sound it out as I write it. */w-ŏ-n/*

The teacher writes *won* on the board.

What does this say? */w-ŏ-n/* *won*

How do we usually say it? */wən/*

Let's add the word *won* to our Lazy Vowel Chart.

Teacher Tip

Schwa /ə / usually sounds like /ŭ/ as in p<u>o</u>lite or <u>a</u>bout. Occasionally schwa may sound like /ĭ/ as in pr<u>e</u>cise.

High Frequency Words

Word Slap

80.2 High Frequency Words – pages 227-228

Cut out the words. Lay 4-8 words out on the table. Read a word. Ask the student to slap the correct one.

Scissors

Handwriting

Handwriting Practice

80.3 Handwriting – page 229

This handwriting sheet is optional. Ask the student to read the sentence aloud before writing it.

Challenge

Dictate the sentence aloud for the student to write on a separate sheet of paper or on her whiteboard.

Reading

Reader

Take out Reader 8. Ask the student to read the title.

Reader 8

> *My Best Game*
> What do you think this book will be about?
>
> Do you play a sport?
> Have you ever played in a game?
> What was your best game?

When the book is finished, ask the student to retell the story.

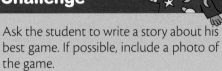

Challenge

Ask the student to write a story about his best game. If possible, include a photo of the game.

REVIEW H

Area	Skill	Mastery
Phonemic Awareness	Rhyme words.	1
Handwriting	Copy a sentence with an uppercase letter and punctuation.	2
Phonograms	Read tch, ow, ou, ough.	1
	Read ea, oa.	2
Reading	Read and comprehend simple sentences.	2
	Read words which include phonograms that have multiple sounds.	2
	Read one-syllable words ending in Y.	2

Skills with a 1 should be mastered before students move on to Foundations Level C. For skills marked with a 2, students should demonstrate familiarity but not necessarily answer all the questions correctly. These skills will be practiced extensively in Level C.

Phonemic Awareness Assessment

Rhyming

H.1 Rhyming – page 230

Read the word. Draw a line to the picture that rhymes with it.

Handwriting Assessment

Handwriting

H.2 Handwriting – page 231

Choose your favorite line size. Read the sentence, then write it.

Phonogram Assessment

Phonogram Assessment

Ask the student to read each of the following phonogram cards: tch, ow, ou, ough, ea, oa.

Basic Phonogram Flash Cards tch, ow, ou, ough, ea, oa

What's That Phonogram?

Highlighter

H.3 What's That Phonogram? – pages 232-233

On your page are groups of four phonograms. I will say a phonogram's sound(s). Color the phonogram with your highlighter.

1. /ō/ two-letter /ō/ that you may not use at the end of English words.
2. /ch/ three-letter /ch/
3. /ē-ĕ-ā/
4. /ŏ-ō-ö-ow-ŭf-ŏf/
5. /ow-ō-ö-ŭ/
6. /ow-ō/

Reading Assessment

Reading

H.4 Matching – pages 234-235

Read the sentence. Match it to the correct picture.

High Frequency Words

H.5 High Frequency Words – page 236

Read each word.

Practice Ideas

Rhyming

"Rhyming" on page 200 in the Teacher's Manual

Handwriting

Using the Tactile Cards, reteach how to write any of the phonograms that are difficult. Break down each step and have the student repeat the short, bold directions aloud.

"Optional Blind Writing" on page 40
"Phonogram Baseball" on page 54
"Phonogram Challenge" on page 75
"Sensory Writing" on page 148
"Finger Painting" on page 164
"Phonogram Race" on page 184

Phonograms

High Frequency Words

Reading

Index

V

Vocabulary
   back (words with multiple meanings) 60
   bike (words with multiple meanings) 102
   breve 2
   pay/paid 202, 204
   personification 89
   say/said 202

Voiced and unvoiced sounds 9, 87

Vowels 1, 4, 57, 148, 154, 160, 175
   Broad 148, 154, 160, 163, 176
   Long 3, 4, 17, 36, 45, 57, 80, 95, 96, 104, 110, 127, 160, 163
   Short 2, 4, 17, 36, 45, 57, 80, 95, 127, 154, 160, 163, 176

W

was 189

what 185

won 218

Y

you 184, 194